C000243443

MY MOTHER
a broken bond

Krystyna Bracey

Grosvenor House
Publishing Limited

This book is published by
Grosvenor House Publishing Ltd
Link House
140 The Broadway, Tolworth, Surrey, KT6 7HT.
www.grosvenorhousepublishing.co.uk

A CIP record for this book
is available from the British Library

ISBN 978-1-80381-325-7

To my son Liam and husband Jeff

With many thanks for all your love and support
in my quest to write this book.

Prologue

From an early age I was made very aware that I had been adopted. That I was a chosen child. This could have never been denied as I had plenty of memories of the children's home I had once lived in.

All my life the word 'adopted' played a central part of my upbringing, it was a constant reminder of how 'lucky' I was. Whilst I appreciated the family I was adopted into, there were many uncomfortable issues that surfaced and with these issues came a strong desire to find answers. However, there would be many twists and turns in my story before I would finally discover what I longed to know.

Who I really was.

Chapters

1) Life begins   1
2) Introducing Barbara and Bill   7
3) Call me darling   12
4) Adoption and a chance discovery   17
5) Teenage years   21
6) Elopement and a disastrous marriage   29
7) Starting afresh   40
8) Laughter and Tears   46
9) Re-adjustment   56
10) Love's Escape   64
11) Trials and Tribulations   71
12) Exits and Entrances   89
13) A far-reaching tale!   96
14) World War II - The Szafranska Story   103
15) A long-awaited meeting   112
16) Footsteps in the past   120
17) Understanding Krysia   129
18) Krysia's secrets   138
19) A journey's end   144
20) Epilogue - What happened next   154

Chapter 1

Life begins

I have struggled for some time to work out where to start with my story!

Should I start from the beginning of my existence, or do I start from my birth mother's existence? My life has taken so many twists and turns it is hard to decide which route to take.

My life began not long after post-war London had endured a terrifying four days of unrelenting, choking smog. The Great Smog of December 1952.

My entry into the world was not heralded by any great celebration. There was no family awaiting the news of my arrival.

It seems my mother was reluctant to acknowledge my existence to anyone, least of all her own family.

I wish I could know what passed between her and me. She was a new mother, and I was a newborn baby. Was my father aware of my birth? Did my mother struggle in giving birth to me, or was my journey into the world an easy one? Was she excited by the prospect of my birth? Was she afraid of the enormous responsibility of bringing up a child? There are so many questions that I would like to ask but which will probably remain unanswered forever.

I was born in St. Stephen's Hospital, Fulham, on 30th December 1952, and my birth mother registered my birth a week later in the Borough of Kensington and Chelsea. She named me Krystyna. This name would later prove to be my only clue when searching for my birth origins.

On 15th January 1953, my birth mother booked herself into Kingsmead, a mother and baby home at Dovehouse Street, London. She gave her name as Krystyna Franska and completed documentation that professed her to be married but separated. She claimed that she had no knowledge of the whereabouts of her husband, Andre, who was an artist. Krystyna stated that she was a fashion designer. She gave her religion as Roman Catholic. This information was to lead to much confusion for all those concerned in making decisions about my future.

After staying overnight at the mother and baby home, Krystyna disappeared, leaving me abandoned. Abandoned for a reason I still have not discovered.

I would love to know what happened during those first few precious days when she fed, clothed, and cared for me. What caused her to make the decision to sever her bond with me?

Despite the hope that Krystyna might return to the home to claim me, this did not happen, which meant a search was initiated to find her. She had not signed me over for adoption, so my future was uncertain.

Because my mother had professed her religion to be Roman Catholic, the Church authorities insisted that, when the time came to re-home me, I should be placed with a Catholic family. I now understand that no amount of persuasion by Social Services was ever going to change this.

Despite much searching for my mother by the authorities, including the Police, it soon became evident that my mother had not been very truthful about her circumstances. It seems there were several discrepancies in the forms filled out by Krystyna.

Following World War 2, the Children Act of 1948 re-organised children's services into the care of local authorities. This meant that fostering or adoption of a child was a good way of dealing with children who were abandoned or orphaned and placed in care. As a consequence of this, I was placed into the care of the London County Council.

Usually, children under two years of age were eagerly sought by would-be parents. There was certainly no shortage of married couples who, for various reasons, were unable to have a child of their own, so would seek a baby that could be fostered or adopted. For reasons unknown to me, I seemed to slip this particular net! This could have been because the authorities involved had to establish that my family could not be found and, therefore, could not confirm that they wanted me to be placed for adoption. Consequently, I had to remain in care.

My situation was not helped by the fact that much of my infancy was spent in and out of hospitals due to illness. I was transferred to various nurseries within the London area following my recovery.

I have often thought that, apart from plenty of paperwork, there is no photographic evidence of me as a baby or toddler, which is rather sad.

In May 1954, because of the Catholic Church's intervention, I was removed from the care of London County Council and transferred into the care of North

Devon County Council. They believed that I would benefit from being sent to the countryside (this was according to paperwork that I was to discover later in life). So, from about eighteen months of age, I was placed in Westmead Children's Home in the small village of Braunton, on the north coast of Devon. This was where my life was set on course for the future.

Westmead was a large, Victorian colonial-style building with several generous rooms downstairs and dormitory-style rooms on the upper floor, which were reached by a sweeping staircase with large windows that overlooked the front garden area. The garden had a sandpit and floral beds, to the side of which was a long, winding driveway.

I cannot recall much of those institutional days. I do have a distinct memory of a large, airy room with brown linoleum flooring that seemed to squeak as you walked across it. A long wooden table ran for what seemed the length of the room. In this room, I would often find myself drawn to a corner; this was my way of feeling a sense of security.

I was described by the authorities as a 'skinny' child with a sallow complexion. My dark brown hair was cut short with a fringe that met my equally dark brown eyes. I had a shy and nervous disposition, and after several months of nursery life with other children, I was regarded as 'backward'. It was deemed that I was not a well-developed child and found socialising with my peers difficult. The exception was a little boy called Roy. He and I often played together and took great delight in playing in the sandpit. One day, I must have been unhappy about something because I hit him with my spade. For this misdemeanour, I was marched into the house and left in my bed upstairs, away from the other children. This was the only time I recall being punished. My friendship with Roy survived this upset, and we continued to play together.

I can vividly recall a Christmas at the home. We all sat against the wall of the main room with the long, wooden table running through the centre. This was my first sight of Father Christmas. I wasn't aware of who Father Christmas was, but I was happy to find this man, clothed in a long coat of red, trimmed with white fur and a hood over his head, coming towards my fellow peers and me with a big tin of sweets. We were each allowed to put our hand into the tin and draw out a handful of smarties. I think my love of sweets started at this point! This is the only memory I have of Christmas at the home. I cannot even recall seeing a Christmas tree or any other sort of festive decoration.

From time to time, there would be an array of visitors to Westmead. These visitors would often stop and talk to the children who would interact with them, but I found it difficult, which meant that I was a bit of a loner.

One day, a lady and gentleman came to visit, and I found myself sitting at a table having tea and cake with them. This happened on several successive occasions, and I began to look forward to seeing them. They were nice people and were always kind and friendly towards me. On each occasion, after tea, I would climb down from my chair and collect a hand brush and pan. I would then clean up the crumbs from the table and under the chair. When asked why I did this, my reply was, "because Matron says we have to sweep up our crumbs".

In the summer of 1956, Matron was standing beside me at the top of the staircase as we looked down the driveway. I recall holding her hand nervously and clutching a doll under my arm along with a book and pencil. I felt a degree of confusion and apprehension as I sensed that something was about to happen. As we descended the wide staircase, we came face to face with the two people who were to become my foster parents. When I saw their faces, I recognised them as the lady and gentleman I had had tea with on so many occasions. They were accompanied by the Area Children's officer, as she had brought the couple called Barbara and Bill to collect me and take me to their home. It all seemed very bewildering with so many faces looking down on me.

Suddenly, Matron was saying goodbye to me as Barbara took my hand, and together with Bill, we walked to the large black car sitting outside.

I recall looking back over my shoulder as I sat in the back seat of the car with Barbara and watched Westmead slowly disappear from view.

I was on my way to a new destiny.

Chapter 2

Introducing Barbara and Bill

Barbara met Bill in the early Spring of 1951. They were both working at the Britannia Hotel in Ilfracombe, North Devon.

Barbara was an attractive lady with shoulder-length wavy, deep auburn hair. Her fair complexion was complemented by her lovely grey-green eyes. Barbara was one of a family of ten siblings. Following the Second World War, during which Barbara had served in the ATS, she had returned to her family home in Fremington. Not wishing to burden her mother, who was still bringing up her four youngest siblings, she gained employment in various hotels and restaurants in both North and South Devon. Barbara became engaged to Ken, a master baker from Combe Martin. Following almost six years of engagement, Barbara's life was turned upside down when Bill entered her life.

Bill was an Irish man who was born in Limerick, Southern Ireland. Having lost both his mother and sister to sudden unforeseen death, he left Ireland to be near to his only surviving sibling; an older brother called Ivan, who lived in Woolacombe, near Ilfracombe.

Bill was a tall, handsome man with blonde hair and piercing blue eyes set in a tanned complexion. He had taken employment as a barman at the Britannia Hotel and met Barbara, who was a live-in waitress. There was an immediate attraction between them. Despite Barbara's engagement to Ken, she could not resist meeting with Bill and, they soon realised they wanted to be together.

Bill decided to return to London. Although his brother was settled in Devon, Bill preferred the hustle and bustle of city life. His only hesitation was his reluctance to leave Barbara. He told the landlady of a nearby pub that he was so in love with Barbara, he was going to ask her to marry him, which is exactly what he did. Barbara was delighted when Bill proposed to her. She loved this new man in her life, with his soft-lilting Irish voice full of charm. She decided there and then that she wanted to be with Bill for the rest of her life.

Barbara told her mother and the rest of the family that she had broken off her engagement to Ken, as she intended to marry Bill. Her mother was not at all amused and told her quite plainly, that she was making a mistake getting involved with a foreigner and a Catholic at that! However, when 'Mama' met Bill, she was very taken with his 'lovely manners' and considerate ways, but the fact remained that he was 'Irish'. She still felt that Barbara should honour her original engagement to marry Ken.

Ken was distraught and begged Barbara to reconsider, but she spurned his attempts to win her back. She had been disenchanted with Ken for some time and was beginning to feel trapped by the sheer length of their engagement and no talk of marriage. Bill gave her a sense of excitement and adventure that she had not felt for a long time.

Once Bill returned to London, he began to make arrangements for Barbara to join him. Whilst he was away, he wrote to Barbara every day. One of the many letters that he sent her was one dated 22nd August 1951, which read:

Dearest B,

A few more lines, have been to see the people of the Cock Hotel, job no use, you would have to cook about 16 luncheons per day, the hours were from 7.30 a.m. until 7.00 p.m., Sunday off - that would not be of any use to us, so we can forget about that. What a life you would have to put up with darling, in a job like that. They don't state the proper duties in their advert. I am anxious to hear from you dear, there are a lot of jobs in the paper this morning that I am sure you would like. I've written to a few, one in particular I may get an answer to. Ivan (Bill's brother) will get in touch with you soon. What do you think of the suggestion about coming here for the week? Write soon dear. It won't be long now, as soon as I have something definite I shall let you know. Thinking of you dear, love always, Bill xxxx p.s. have got to get to work dear, excuse short letter'.

Barbara loved receiving Bill's letters and would read them over and over again. Because of the strained atmosphere that prevailed at home following her break-up with Ken, she was anxious to move to London as soon as Bill could find them both somewhere to live. A job offer arose for a couple to manage the Rose and

Crown pub in Hammersmith. At last, this allowed Barbara to head to London and join Bill. Barbara was really excited when she travelled to London at the end of August so that she and Bill could start to make plans for their future. Because Bill was a practising Catholic, he asked Barbara if she was willing to take instruction in his faith so that they could marry in the Catholic church. She agreed to do this but would not convert to his faith. On 29th September 1951, with just two of Barbara's sisters present, and Bill's brother Ivan, they were married at Holy Trinity Church, Hammersmith. Despite the rationing that still existed following the Second World War, Barbara had managed to save enough coupons for her wedding trousseau and to celebrate with a small reception after the wedding.

Barbara enjoyed the hospitality trade. She loved the thrill of meeting several well-known theatre stars because the Rose and Crown pub was near the King's Theatre. However, after two years, she was still unable to adapt to city life and yearned to return to Devon. Bill accepted that Barbara was unhappy, so they moved back to be near her family. They stayed with Barbara's mother in Fremington whilst looking for their first house.

They were eventually given the opportunity of renting a council house just a short distance from her mother. They were delighted to have their own home. As time passed, Barbara began to sense that motherhood was not on the horizon. She was very disappointed, especially as two of her sisters already had children. She loved being an aunty but longed to be a mother. One day Barbara read an advert in the local paper for a widower who was looking for someone to care for his small son whilst he was at work. With Bill's support, Barbara wrote to him, but someone had already been found. This left Barbara feeling very dejected.

A few weeks later, Barbara and Bill were approached by Devon County Children's Department and asked if they would consider fostering a child. It had come to their attention that they had sought to look after the widower's son. Barbara and Bill were initially apprehensive about this sort of commitment. It was quite different to look after a child during the day and hand him back to their parent in the evening. Fostering would be a much greater commitment.

The Area Children's Officer, a Mrs. Isobel Dashwood visited them. A short while after, Barbara and Bill found themselves standing in the entrance hall of Westmead Childrens' Home. Mrs Dashwood told them that she had a particular child in mind that could dearly do with some real love and one-to-one care. When they first saw the child in question, she was sitting alone in the corner of a large room watching several children running around, shouting and playing.

Barbara and Bill were filled with emotion at the sight of the small, peaky looking child sucking her fingers and rocking herself in a chair.

That child was me.

Chapter 3

Call me darling

My journey to Beachfield Road, Fremington, was a long one. Apart from being taken out for an occasional walk into the village of Braunton with the other children from the home, I had never travelled very far from Westmead. Now I was suddenly sitting in a big car, and it felt strange. Fields and trees flashed past my eyes as I stared out of the window. Barbara was clutching my hand quite tightly as if to reassure me that everything was alright.

Finally, we reached what was to be my new home. It was a pebble-dashed council house set in the corner of a small cul-de-sac. The approach to it was by way of a footpath set at an angle to the house, at the side of which was a pretty blossom tree full of pink clusters of flowers, a memory I vividly recall.

As I entered the house, I came face to face with a chirping budgerigar. I was immediately fascinated by the little bird with its bright blue chest, striped black and white wings, and small yellow beak.

Bill took great pleasure in introducing me to 'Kim', and then he and Barbara showed me around my new home. It was an average-sized house with a large kitchen overlooking a long back garden. There was a big sitting room furnished with a three-piece suite and dining table and chairs. There were windows at each end, which looked out to the front and rear gardens. It was a pleasing, comfortable room, complete with a beige tiled fireplace. Upstairs were three bedrooms, one of which was to be mine. My bedroom walls were decorated with daisy patterned paper, and there was a large bed, beside which was a small, green cot for my one and only doll, which I had brought from Westmead. It was a sad-looking doll with two arms but only one leg!

It was all very strange to me as I had only ever been used to dormitory style sleeping arrangements, and now I was faced with a double bed with pretty patterned bedding. The dressing table, which sat in front of the window, was deep brown in colour with a large mirror. I caught sight of myself in the mirror and started giggling. It was the first time I had seen myself in a mirror. I had a happy time as I explored each room of the house, including the bathroom.

My surroundings were a far cry from what I had experienced at Westmead. As I settled into my new home, I had to learn to get out of the habit of knocking on each door before I entered, whether it was the kitchen or sitting room. When 'mummy', as I began to call Barbara, asked me why I kept knocking on each door, I replied that Matron told me to do this when I was at Westmead. I recall being enfolded into Barbara's arms as she told me that it was not necessary to do this anymore. One day, when Barbara called my name to come downstairs, I asked, "Why don't you call me darling?". This was what I had often been called by the staff at Westmead. She laughed at me and said, "Well, I won't be calling you darling, your name is Krystyna".

My mother took great pleasure in dressing me in lovely clothes, many of which she made by hand. She was a clever seamstress and a very good knitter. I had never had such an array of clothes to choose from and took great care of everything I wore.

My mother's family was a large one, so I instantly became the niece of several aunts and uncles and gained several cousins. My mother's mother was a really lovely lady whom I affectionately called 'Granny'. She was a wonderful, patient lady who had curly, soft white hair, which was always kept in place by a fine net. I loved spending time with her and listening to her tales about my uncles and aunties when they were children. She told me that Barbara could be a naughty girl at times, which amused me. My time spent with Granny was very special, and she probably helped make me feel more secure about my new life. She liked to share her household chores with me, such as on a Monday morning, I would help her put the white, heavy cotton sheets through the mangle and then turn the handle. In the height of summer, when the fruit in Granny's garden was abundant, she would often give me the task of picking gooseberries or black currants, all of which would then be bottled in Kilner jars, ready for the winter. My reward for such tasks would be 'horse's teeth', which were crusts of bread cut into wide strips, and spread liberally with butter and delicious homemade jam. I think, looking back, that Granny was trying to feed me up as I was a skinny child with long, lanky legs.

Occasionally, whilst at Granny's, aunts, uncles and cousins would visit. One cousin, Steven, was a near neighbour to us at Beachfield Road, and he and I would often play in each other's house or garden. Together we used to visit a fellow neighbour, called Mr. Sam, and his wife, Mrs.Ruby. They had an Airedale dog named Chum, and we loved playing with him.

Life, in general, was quite good and a far cry from the institutional life of my early years. During my foster years, Devon County Council oversaw the process of my impending adoption, as this was Barbara and Bill's ultimate goal in fostering me. This meant that the Area Children's Officer, Mrs. Dashwood, would visit me at home, and in turn, Barbara and I would visit her in Victoria Chambers, the Area Office based in the High Street of the nearby town of Barnstaple. Mrs. Dashwood was a tall, handsome woman with a kind, open face who was always smartly dressed in a suit. She would chat to me generally about little things such as my time at home and admire what I was wearing. I was very proud of my clothes, and I know that Barbara took great pride in dressing me well.

The effects of my early years in institutional life had left me with some speech issues and, according to the Educational Psychologist, I was regarded as being of "low intelligence". He also stated that I was easily distracted and could lose interest in things quickly. Unfortunately, these comments were to haunt me for quite some time. Despite all the good things in my life, there was a subtle undercurrent of abuse towards me by Barbara. I was too young to understand that this was the case. One day I had accidentally dirtied my pants, and by way of punishment, she rubbed my face in them and then told me to wash them. I soon became frightened of my mother's occasional menacing look and would nervously do as I was told. Another example of her abuse was when I accidentally tore a dress I was to wear, and having asked her what dress to put on in its place she told me that I could wear my father's old work shirt and a pair of play trousers. She went on to say that by doing this, I would then be like the 'poor children' who never had nice clothes to wear. I remember standing in front of her feeling very sad and bewildered as I stood wearing my father's old shirt that was far too big and nearly reached my feet! I recall sobbing loudly and feeling quite wretched at her treatment of me. Barbara laughed at me but finally relented and found me an alternative dress to wear. It was a moment that has stayed with me forever.

Such experiences as these taught me to remain quiet and not incur any wrath from her. There were occasions, too, when she would just slap me across the face or head if I did not duck quickly enough. I began to realise that these instances only occurred when my father was not around. I found it hard to understand why my mother could be so nice for much of the time but so cruel at others.

I was to live with this sort of erratic behaviour from Barbara for the rest of her life. I never told anyone about this, not even 'Daddy'.

Chapter 4

Adoption and a chance discovery

In October 1957, it was decided by the Children's Officer, Mrs. Dashwood, in consultation with Barbara and Bill, that I should start attending school. It was a newly-built school in Fremington, and as I was then the youngest pupil at the school, I was chosen to make a presentation to the wife of the chairman of Devon County Education Committee on the official opening of the school. Barbara and Bill were delighted that I had been chosen for this honour. I recall nervously curtsying as I presented the bouquet of flowers to Mrs. Lampard-Vachell.

I enjoyed being at school and socialising with my fellow peers, but it soon became evident that I was not the best of scholars. I found myself being reprimanded by my mother after she was told that I was not paying attention during lessons. My mother was also annoyed that I was not proficient in talking to people. She would tell me that I should "talk properly" and that if I did not begin to do well at school, she would send me back to 'the home'. This threat hung over me for many of my early years. I eventually went to see a speech therapist who turned to my mother and said that I did not have a problem; I was just lazy! Obviously, this comment did not go down well with Barbara. She began to make me repeat little verses like 'how now brown cow' so that I would enunciate the words properly. She was sensitive about the criticism cast at me and began making spiteful remarks to me about my birth mother, saying that I had 'foreign' blood and that I would end up like her!

Shortly before I was officially adopted, Barbara and Bill took me to the Catholic Church in Barnstaple where I was christened into the Catholic faith. I recall the priest, Father Lynch, saying to me, "You are too big for me to lift up to the font, so I will have to christen you standing". This caused a trickle of laughter among the small congregation who had assembled for the event. My Godmother was Mrs. Hanafin who ran the Fox & Hounds pub in Fremington. She and her husband had given a reference for Barbara and Bill when they first sought to foster me.

In July 1958, I was formally adopted by Barbara and Bill, and they officially became Mummy and Daddy, as I called them. The Judge who granted the adoption asked my parents if they would like to change my name, Krystyna, to one of their own personal choice. They declined, saying that my name had been given to me at birth by my biological mother and they would keep it. My father decided to give me a middle name, Theresa, which had been his late mother's name. I was to discover much later just how much of a coincidence this was!

From here on, my mother would often remind me that I was very fortunate to have been 'chosen' by her and Bill. At that time, I had no conception of my having another mother; it had not yet dawned on me just what it meant to be adopted.

I began to question what was really happening in my life and why I was being treated with kindness one minute but nastiness the next. I started to wish I would be found one day by my 'proper' mother.

I only stayed at the school at Fremington for a short while as we moved from Beachfield Road to another council house in Sticklepath near Barnstaple. One day my father announced that I would be going to a school run by nuns. I misunderstood what he said and started to cry saying, "I don't want to go to a school run by gnomes".

St. Mary's School in Barnstaple was a Catholic school immediately adjacent to the Catholic Church where I had been baptised. It was a small school run by a handful of nuns and a couple of lay teachers. My days there were happy and fairly content. My school work began to show promise, and my parents were pleased with my progress.

During the school holidays, my mother would leave me at home while she went to work for a couple of hours. She would encourage me to stay in my bedroom, telling me that I could read or play with my toys. I was naive at the time about being left alone in the house at such a young age. I thought that children were often left on their own!

One day, when I was about ten, being a curious child, I seized the opportunity of going to the sideboard in the sitting room. I knew that this was where my mother had a beautiful, camel skin handbag which my uncle had brought back to her after the war, as a present from Egypt. The bag had always fascinated me with its pale, soft camel skin embossed with pictures of pyramids and palm trees. I cannot explain what really drew me to the bag, but I wanted to see what was inside. I was initially disappointed as I did not find a great deal, but suddenly

I came across a small envelope on which my mother had written my name. I opened the flap and took out a piece of paper, which read 'Adoption Order'. The paper revealed my real surname, Franska, my first name, Krystyna, and another name, Andrea. I was stunned; my mouth went dry. I had a sister! I put the paper back in its envelope and closed the bag. I was staggered by what I had just discovered and rushed upstairs as tears came into my eyes. I threw myself on my bed, crying and saying to myself, "I have a sister, I have a sister".

One of the many stories that my mother used to tell me about my adoption was that she thought I could be one of a twin! How she came to this conclusion, I do not know, but having discovered the paperwork revealing the two names, Krystyna and Andrea, I now believed that this was true.

Chapter 5

Teenage years

I never revealed to anyone what I had found that day when I had been left alone in the house, but I carried it constantly in my mind. Whenever I read a newspaper or magazine, I would scour the pages in search of the surname I had discovered. I would even watch the credits at the end of films, or 'fil-ums', as my father used to call them in his soft Irish voice. I was always searching for the name that would lead me to discovering my real parents, but it remained elusive. As time passed, I began to wonder more and more about my birth and more so, about my lost twin sister! The evidence that I had discovered convinced me that I had one.

As life moved forward, my mother's subtle cruelty continued, either by physical or mental abuse, but never openly, so my father remained oblivious.

I recall being made to feel very inadequate when I failed my eleven plus exam to enter the Grammar School in Barnstaple. Barbara was horrified at the thought that I would have to attend the Secondary Modern school. To avoid this humiliation, she insisted that having been brought up in the Catholic faith and having attended a junior Catholic school, I should be sent to St. Joseph's Convent in Barnstaple. This meant that my parents would have to pay school fees, but as I was a Catholic, they were granted a small bursary to assist with the expense. Looking back, I feel sure that my mother derived a certain pleasure in showing off and saying that her daughter attended a 'private' school. I loved my time at the Convent and wore my uniform of gold, blue and cream with pride. I particularly liked the blue felt hat with a gold and blue band that I would wear with my winter uniform, but I was not so fond of the straw boater that had to be worn with the mustard coloured dress in the summer. The nuns at the Convent were very patient people, and I was struck by the fact that they always seemed to have an air of peace about them. I excelled at subjects such as Art, English and Science. Sister Geraldine was one of my favourite teachers; she taught Science and Biology. I recall being fascinated by her habit of nibbling the chalk sticks she used on the blackboard.

Once a week, as part of our school curriculum, we would attend Chapel. This meant having to walk via a pathway that led from the school to the boarders' accommodation, where the Chapel was situated. This walk would also act as a 'nature' ramble when we would be expected to spot various plants as part of our biology lesson. I experienced a certain sense of tranquillity when visiting the Chapel and found myself drawn by the quiet awe of contemplation.

I had several classmates with whom I got on well, but sadly I did not see them out of school. I felt very conscious that living on a Council estate meant that friends in my peer group were non-existent. So once again, apart from seeing Granny, my time at weekends or school holidays would largely be spent on my own.

I would wander the surrounding neighbourhood and imagine what was happening in the various houses and bungalows I passed.

Most of the pupils in my class were aware that I was adopted and that I had no siblings. Surprisingly, there was only one of my friends who, like me, was an only child. One day, wanting to seek some attention from my fellow peers, I made up a tale that I had a long lost brother who had been found living in America. I went on to say that he would be coming over to meet me! I revelled in the interest that my friends began to show, so I continued with the lie. When asked what my brother's name was, I instantly replied Richard. Little did I know then that 'Richard' really existed! I never got caught out by this tale as in February 1967, shortly after my fourteenth birthday, I had to leave the convent because my father had been made redundant due to the cuts to the railway branches by Dr. Beeching. Subsequently because of the lack of employment in the area, my parents made the decision to move away, taking a council house exchange to Trowbridge in Wiltshire. My father felt that there would be greater opportunities for work there.

I was really sad to leave the convent and still have the farewell card that my friends made for me. Sister Geraldine gave me a luminous cross to hang on my wall, and this too, has remained with me throughout the years.

The day we moved was a strange day indeed. In order to save expense on travel, my father made arrangements for us to journey in the back of the removal lorry. The last piece of furniture to go into the lorry was the settee. We sat for four hours in complete darkness as we travelled towards our new home and a new destiny. When we finally reached our destination, I ran down the pathway to the house, and immediately my heart sank at its outward appearance. The house was in a row of dull red-bricked buildings and, in the rain, it looked forlorn and sad. Inside, the house was spacious, but the general decor left a bit to be desired. I could tell my parents were very disappointed in their exchange, so much so that my mother said they would strive to move from there as soon as possible. It was certainly a stark contrast to the house we had left behind.

In addition to my disappointment about the house, I soon discovered that, within the town one's nostrils were constantly met with the pervading smell of hops brewing at the local brewery and the horrendous smell of the neighbouring meat factory. It was a far cry from the smells of the Devonshire countryside!

To add to my misery, my parents told me that I would have to attend the local Secondary school because there was no longer a convent that offered schooling in the town. This was a big shock for me. To move from the tranquil way of school life in a convent to a comprehensive school was a particularly upsetting ordeal.

As if my world had not already been turned upside down enough, I was confronted with the long-kept secret of my father's diabetes. One day, I became aware that he was slurring his speech and acting as if he were drunk. My mother gave me instructions on how to care for my father if he became ill in the future. I later learned that my father had been diabetic since I was first fostered. Whilst fostering me, he had been worried that this would impede my adoption, but this was not the case.

Each Sunday, I would attend our local Catholic Church mainly with my father, but sometimes on my own. I had made friends at school with a Polish girl called Sabina, who lived quite near me. One day she asked me to go with her to the Polish mass, and I readily agreed. The Polish mass was early each Sunday morning, and although I could not understand the language, I felt drawn to it in a strange way. I was fascinated by the way the congregation gathered together and were so friendly towards each other. Usually, when leaving the English service, you came out as you went in, on your own. This was not the case with the Polish people. They would greet you in a warm manner, and even hug you on occasion as they said, "Dzien dobry" (good morning). Sadly, my newfound Sunday enjoyment was brought to an abrupt end. My mother asked me one Sunday why I was going to church so early. I replied that as I was going with Sabina, my Polish friend, and that we were attending the Polish mass. On hearing this, my mother rounded on me, calling me names and saying, "You are a 'yes' girl. You would drink a cup of poison if you were told to". With her face full of anger, she said, "I'm warning you, do you want to end up like an old Polish washerwoman? You will if you don't stay away from them. You are looking for trouble". I didn't know what to say or how to react. Was she afraid of something?

Barbara had often told me that she believed my birth parents were Polish or Austrian, but now she was acting in a hostile manner. She told me that I was to attend the 'proper' Catholic mass and that she would know if I defied her. I was so disappointed and felt that although I was approaching my fifteenth year, I was being treated like a child.

As if life had not changed enough for me, my mother began full-time employment at a food factory. Suddenly,

I was faced with going to school and returning each day to an empty house. As my mother's working hours were different to my father's, I had to take on a number of household chores, including preparing and starting the evening meal each day. As a consequence of this, the relationship between my mother and me became deeply strained, and I found myself feeling very unhappy at her continual, critical attitude towards me.

My parents managed to leave the council estate that we had moved to within six months. They both worked very hard and finally achieved buying a small terraced house. It was a lovely, spacious house inside with a medium-sized garden to the rear. Each morning one was greeted with the smell of freshly baked bread as the house backed onto the local bakery. I loved going to the shop each day to choose a loaf of bread, sometimes a cottage loaf, and sometimes a bloomer, and now and again, a plain tin loaf. All these things I remember with a certain fondness.

My school days turned out to be a form of escape from the unhappiness I now felt at home. Although we now had a dog, Pip, a miniature silver grey poodle whom I doted on, my days were filled with a sense of gloom at the prospect of how my mother would be when she returned home from work each evening. Sometimes she would be pleasant and caring, but at other times was fault-finding.

We did have some enjoyable times as a family. My father would often book a coach trip to Bath or Bristol and occasionally even go on a 'mystery tour'. I loved these occasions, but there was always a fear that a wrong word here or there would lead to dissension and the usual criticism of whatever I had said or done.

On one occasion, on a dark winter's night, my mother had sent me out to the shops for some washing powder. I was feeling particularly down within myself. Things always seemed to be going wrong, and even though I set out to fetch the shopping, I decided there and then to run away.

I really didn't know where to go; I was so miserable. I attempted to seek sanctuary at a nearby convent for retired nuns. As I stood on the doorstep of the nunnery ringing the doorbell, my misery overcame me, and I started to cry uncontrollably. A nun opened the door and, seeing the state I was in, took me into a small room with several religious artefacts on the surrounding walls. The nun told me to sit down whilst she went to fetch me a glass of water. When she returned, she chatted to me in a gentle manner and, eventually, having composed myself, I poured my woeful story out to her. She asked me how old I was and, although she sympathised with me, she told me that in no way could I leave home. Her words were comforting, and I realised she was right; there was no way I could just run away. She said, "God will protect you, my dear. Go home and pray, He will give you the strength that you need". I had calmed down and began to feel embarrassed and stupid at what I had done. I apologised for the trouble I had caused, and prepared to return home. The nun said that she was only too pleased that I had chosen to go back, as opposed to anywhere else. She said that I was in a vulnerable state because of how I was feeling. She advised me to talk to my parents when I got home, but that was something I knew I would never do. To my surprise, she insisted on walking me home, presumably to ensure that I did just that. As I approached my front door, I thanked her again for her help. She replied, "Bless you, look after yourself".

As I opened the front door, my mother met me and shouted, "Where on earth have you been?". I muttered an excuse saying that because I could not find the particular soap powder she wanted, I had walked into Trowbridge town. She said that she was beginning to get worried and that Bill was about to go out looking for me. I suddenly felt guilty at what I had done, but nothing further was said.

I took myself to bed that night and, feeling thoroughly miserable, turned over and cried into my pillow. I felt distraught about everything in life.

Chapter 6

Elopement and a disastrous marriage

After my madcap idea of running away from home, life continued much as it had before. Some days my mother was kind and attentive; other days, she showed signs of aggression and would be critical of me in every sense of the word. My school work suffered because I began to play truant. It wasn't a regular occurrence, just enough to relieve the pressure I was feeling about everything.

Eventually, I left school with sufficient examination passes to enable me to attend Trowbridge Technical College, where I did a secretarial course.

It was whilst I was at college that I learnt to drive. I passed my driving test (on the third attempt) in March 1971. My parents were delighted, and my mother, in particular, was filled with enthusiasm at the prospect of me being able to take the three of us out. There would be no more waiting for buses or trains.

My mother surprised me when, just a few days after passing my test, she took me to a garage to choose my first car, a 1964 cream and blue Ford Anglia. I was wide-eyed with excitement as I watched my parents pay over the princely sum of £150 in cash. I was touched by their generosity and the swiftness of their actions.

I remember the sense of freedom I had when I took my first journey out in the car on my own. I felt liberated.

After leaving college, I found employment as a secretary at a wine and spirits distributor in Trowbridge. I earned £16 a month and was delighted when I received my first salary cheque. Of course, my mother made it very clear that I should pay her 'board and lodge', which I was only too happy to do.

As my parents had been kind enough to buy me my first car, I felt obliged to take them out most weekends. I soon realised that I had made a mistake by doing this. My mother, in particular, became difficult if I made alternative arrangements with friends. It also proved difficult if a boyfriend was on the scene. My mother would become quite manipulative if the friendship went beyond a few weeks. I began to realise that my mother was jealous. It was quite a strain to cope with someone who was sometimes supportive and at other times not. She became more critical about things, such as what I chose to wear or how I wore my hair. She was also hurtful about what she called my 'foreign' look, saying I was beginning to look like an 'old Polish washerwoman'. I never understood how she arrived at this expression about me or how she came to have such a spiteful attitude.

After a particularly difficult weekend with her contrary behaviour, I decided that I was going to leave home. One morning, before leaving for work, I left a note telling my parents that I was moving out.

That night I booked myself into an hotel. My job allowed a staff discount for certain company accommodation, which enabled me to stay there for nearly a week. A few days had passed when my mother came to see me at work. She stood in my office and begged me to return home. She told me that my father had not been well and they both really missed me. Feeling guilty about them both, particularly my father, I relented and returned home. The first words my father said to me as I walked into the house were, "Ah, the prodigal daughter has returned." I was taken back by his coldness; he was normally such a gentle soul. I began to wish I had not returned. The love within me for my parents was being stretched to its limit; one part of me felt guilty, the other part of me wanted to escape again.

I had always had a love of film and theatre and decided to join the local drama group. This was where I met my future husband, Robert.

Robert was a tall, well-built man with very wavy mousey-coloured hair. He wore black thick-rimmed glasses and had what I thought was a charming personality. We started going out regularly, but for some reason, my parents were not happy about my relationship with him. Little did I know at that time that my mother was aware that Robert was already involved with a local girl. She only revealed this to me many years later.

One Sunday evening, I had planned to meet Robert, but my mother started to question why I was going out when I had work the following morning. I couldn't believe that, at 19, I was being treated this way. Even worse was to come when my father said that I was to return home no later than 10 o'clock. I was shocked that he, too, was trying to dictate my life.

When Robert picked me up, my father shouted after me," I'm warning you, you'd better be back by

10 o'clock." On hearing this, Robert said I was being treated like a child and that in no way would he be returning me home by that time. We drove to Bath, where we had a meal. I started looking at my watch and, as I did so, Robert suddenly said, "Let's get married." I was startled by his proposal but, without a second thought, I agreed. It was a crazy moment, but I felt I had had enough, and Robert's proposal was my way of escaping my mother and father's anger, which I could not face.

I gave no thought as to the consequences of this decision. We drove to my house, where I slipped a note through the door saying that I was leaving and getting married to Robert.

We drove to Southampton Airport that same night and the following morning took a flight to Jersey, where Robert lived.

On arrival at Jersey Airport, Robert called his home to arrange for us to be collected.

I was surprised to find that the person who arrived to pick us up was the housekeeper, a lady called Mrs. Lodge. As she drove us to the house, she informed Robert that only his mother was at home. His father was away on business. I sat in the back of the car and was amazed as we turned into a long driveway. It led to a spectacular looking granite-built house, which sparkled in the sunshine. It was surrounded by cedar trees and to the left of the drive was a tennis court. There was also a spectacular view of the sea. It was enough to take one's breath away.

As we stepped into the beautifully carpeted hallway, Robert's mother greeted us, but not in a particularly friendly manner. She was very annoyed that Robert had arrived home unannounced and that he had seemingly abandoned his accountancy studies. She took him into the library, leaving me standing in the hallway. As I looked around, and took in the wide staircase that flowed upwards to deep large windows, I realised what a grand house Robert's family lived in. A short while later, Robert reappeared and said that we would be returning to England on the next available flight. Robert's mother made no effort to acknowledge me. Less than an hour later, we were back at the airport.

It seemed that Robert's idea had not gone according to plan. On arrival at Southampton, we had no option but to drive back to Trowbridge, where I stayed with Robert in his rented accommodation.

Because I had left my job without notice, I now found myself without work. Whilst my employer was sympathetic about my situation, my position had already been filled.

A few days later, I finally summoned the courage to visit my parents with Robert, when we made it very clear that we intended to get married. They were not best pleased about the situation but were relieved to find that I was safe. They realised that I was determined to remain with Robert. My mother surprised me by saying very little, but as we turned to leave, my father said, "Mark my words, Krystyna, you are making a big mistake."

Not knowing what to do next, Robert and I decided to leave Trowbridge. We headed to Plymouth, a place that Robert had visited and liked in the past. We rented a small flat and were both fortunate enough to find work. However, life was far from idyllic. My job did not live up to my expectations, and neither did Robert's. Within a few short weeks of living together, Robert suddenly announced that he had found a position for us in London. Unbeknownst to me, he had applied for us to work as assistant managers at The Wheatsheaf pub in Shepherds Bush. The pub was an old Victorian establishment. Our accommodation would be a bedroom located on the top floor of the building. I remember thinking how strange it was that I should find myself working in the same industry as my parents had when they were newly married.

However, it turned out to be nothing like I had envisaged. As part of my duties, I was told that I would be expected to make breakfast each day for all the staff, of which there were nine including Robert and myself. I was also expected to make the beds for all the live-in staff, which I felt quite uncomfortable about, as one particular member used to suffer badly with body odour!. In addition to this, I had to serve customers in both the public and saloon bars each morning and evening.

We had lied about being married when Robert applied for the job, and after a few weeks, the Tax man caught us out! The manager, who was a brusque Scotsman did not mince his words, threatened us with the loss of our jobs if we did not not do something about it. We hurriedly made arrangements to get married. I had hoped that we might be able to marry at Caxton Hall but we were not resident in the right area. So it was that, on the 10th March 1973, we were married at Hammersmith Registry Office. My parents refused to come to the wedding, which did not surprise me, but some of Robert's family did attend.

It was on this occasion that I realised just how wealthy Robert's family were. His mother had arranged for us to dine at the Savoy hotel after our wedding.

There was no wedding cake or grand speeches, just a very nice meal, plus a cheque for £500. After the meal and a toast with champagne, we all retired to the family suite to relax for the afternoon.

However, Robert relaxed a little too much! So much so that he decided we would not return to work for our designated shift that evening. To cover up, he rang our employer and said that he thought he had a touch of food poisoning. Robert did not think this would be questioned. But a short while later, a knock at the door revealed the manager of the Savoy. He enquired as to a statement that had been made about a possible case of food poisoning. Realising this was due to Robert's cunning plan to avoid work, his mother was highly embarrassed. She apologised profusely to the manager and immediately gave us our marching orders.

This meant we had no alternative but to return to work. Unfortunately, we were unprepared for the hostility we received from some of the staff, including the manager's wife. They were particularly abusive in their manner and, as we made our way upstairs to our room, I was assaulted by one of the staff. I screamed for someone to call the police, which thankfully, they did. Within a short while, I found myself being placed in the back of a police car for safety. Robert tried to follow me but was stopped by the police and told to stay and pack a few of our possessions so that we could find some accommodation for the night. The police assured us that we would be allowed to return the following day to collect the rest of our belongings. It was obvious with what had passed that we would no longer be working at the Wheatsheaf!

With £500 in our pocket, we booked into the Royal Lancaster hotel, just off Hyde Park. We stayed there for a week and decided to treat it as our honeymoon. It had certainly not been a wedding night to remember!

Following this debacle, we soon found alternative employment at another pub, The Duke of Cumberland in Chelsea. It was a much nicer public house, and the managers were very understanding about the situation we had found ourselves in. Sadly though, Robert's work ethics did not prove to be good enough for them. They were more than happy with my efforts, but eventually, we were asked to leave. This meant we would no longer have our live-in accommodation. Because of this, Robert totally lost interest in trying to gain further employment in London. He rang his parents, who agreed that he could return to Jersey to live and that we would, for the time being, live in the family home at St. Brelade.

Whilst living in London, there were many times when I thought about the fact that this was where I had been born. I felt a strong desire to search for my birth parents, but because of my lack of knowledge of how to start such a search, I was unable to do this.

Since I had left home and married, my mother continued to try and exert her control over me, mainly through letters she would send now and again. She often made the point that, in her eyes, I had not married in a 'proper manner'. This was a veiled reference to my Catholic upbringing. She said that she and my father did not accept my marriage and that in order to appease them, I should get the marriage blessed. However, Robert was adamant that this would not happen. His refusal to comply with my parent's wishes meant that my mother was not prepared to accept my husband. In fact, she made it very clear that she disliked him intensely. If I spoke to her on the phone, she would refer to us as 'Beauty and the Beast'. She did not regard Robert as good looking beside her 'beautiful' daughter. To make things worse, when my mother sent me postcards or letters, she always used words such as, 'you know what you must do' at the finish. This did nothing to endear her to Robert.

I had gained employment as a Jersey Civil Servant, and I thoroughly enjoyed this. Despite enjoying some amazing experiences with Robert's family, such as travelling by private jet for lunch in St.Malo or visiting Paris for the weekend, life with Robert was nothing like I had first imagined it would be. He started to be abusive and unkind. I had been longing for a child, but so far this had not happened. One day however, Robert came home and announced that he had told his colleagues at work that I was pregnant! I was astounded and asked him how he thought I could live such a lie. He responded by saying, "Well, you soon will be", and with that, he dragged me into the bedroom as if to prove a point. A few weeks later, I told Robert that I thought I was pregnant. I was sure he would be pleased, but was totally unprepared by his reaction. He turned on me and was full of rage. He started banging the kitchen table with his fist, shouting that I would not be keeping it. I was completely and utterly bewildered by his actions. That same night he raped me so severely that I lost the baby. A few days later, he covered up his lies to his work colleagues by telling them that I had had a miscarriage.

This was not the only time I endured Robert's perverse cruelty; it became such a constant occurrence that I almost took my own life by driving my car off a steep incline just off the airport road leading to St.Aubin.

Something within me suddenly brought me to my senses, and my foot hit the brakes. Instead, I confided in my doctor, who having witnessed Robert's behaviour to me on a particular occasion, advised me to take legal advice. However, this proved pointless, as I was simply told to go away and start a diary of any abusive treatment by Robert in order to build a case of cruelty whereby I might gain a divorce, but this would by no means be a certainty.

I felt desperately alone, I had friends but did not feel I could confide in them, as I felt embarrassed at the thought of admitting my marriage was on the rocks. I felt that there was no way out.

I decided to make a trip to see my parents. I flew to Exeter and hired a car to travel to Bideford, North Devon, where my parents had moved due to my father's ill health. Robert did not wish to accompany me, for which I was very grateful. During my visit, I finally broke down and told my parents how unhappy I was. They were very sympathetic and supportive. My father suggested I leave Robert and return home to them. However, I was uncertain as to exactly how I would be able to do this, and returned to Jersey to work out what I was going to do with my life.

When I arrived back in Jersey, Robert met me at the airport and drove me back to our flat, whereupon he got out of the car and suddenly flung open the garage door to reveal a brand new shiny VW Golf. Before I could register what was happening, Robert said that the car was mine and that I was to take it and leave him. Whilst I had been away, he had arranged to rent a bedroom in our flat to two female lodgers, and he wanted me out. I was stunned and could not believe what he was saying.

Robert told me that our marriage was over, and he wanted me out of his life. I couldn't believe what was happening, even though within me, I felt that I had been given a chance to escape. When Robert left for work the following day, he told me to make arrangements to vacate the flat. I rang my parents and also a solicitor my father had recommended. The solicitor agreed that this would be my best course of action. I immediately went about arranging my departure, and was packed and ready to leave a couple of days later. However, the following morning, due to bad weather, the ferry was cancelled. Robert, who had followed me to the ferry, probably to ensure I really left, suggested I return to the flat overnight. Stupidly I did, only to find that by going back, he took advantage by raping me, after which he said it was my way of thanking him for the car!

Thankfully, the weather had improved the following day, and I was able to take my leave of the island and my unhappy marriage. Whilst on deck, I threw my prescribed bottle of Valium tablets into the swirling waters of the sea. I was finally free of the cruel and manipulative man Robert had turned out to be. I was thankful to be returning home to my parents and a different life.

Chapter 7

Starting afresh

With a huge sigh of relief, I disembarked the ferry from Jersey to Weymouth and made my way to my parents. They were very supportive of my decision to leave Robert and welcomed me home with open arms.

I had already spoken to a solicitor that my father had put me in touch with. When I rang him, he agreed that in the interest of my health and well-being, my best course of action was to return to the mainland. Because of my marriage to a Jersey resident, I was classed as the same. This meant that I could not commence divorce proceedings until I had re-established my English domicile, which would take six months.

Once back with my parents, I initially found employment as a secretary with a firm of solicitors in Barnstaple. I could not believe it when one day, a phone call was received enquiring whether they could represent Robert with regard to divorce proceedings. Of all the solicitors within North Devon, he had chosen my employees! He was not made aware that I was working there, but was advised to seek an alternative solicitor.

A few months later, I left this employment and went to work as a Personnel Assistant at the well-known door manufacturer, Shapland and Petter, based in Barnstaple.

The company at that time was owned by Lord Wavell Wakefield and his family, who were regular visitors to the factory. I thoroughly enjoyed the variety of my work each day. During the course of my time there, I was delighted to have the opportunity of meeting the newly-elected Prime Minister, Margaret Thatcher, and her husband Denis, when she visited the factory during the summer of 1979. I also met Viscount Linley, the son of Princess Margaret, when he paid a visit to tour the factory and also met many of the young apprentices that we employed. Another interesting person who visited the company was Brian Johnston, the presenter of the radio programme, Down Your Way.

As I began to settle into a new way of life, Robert continued to taunt me, albeit from a distance. One day, my mother rang me at work and told me that Robert was looking for me and had been to their house bearing a large bouquet of red roses. My father was not at all impressed and gave him short shrift, telling him to go away and that they did not know where I was. I recall how nervous I was as I sat in my car later that same evening. I was fearful that Robert might still be around, waiting for me to appear. Eventually, I drove home, and was able to heave a sigh of relief; he had gone but left the flowers. Needless to say, much as I like flowers, I threw them away. A few days later, I received a letter from Robert's advocate in Jersey, stating that I was to return the car even though Robert had insisted that it was mine. He now claimed that I had taken it without his permission. I rang my solicitor, who told me to ignore the request. I later received a visit from HM Customs to verify that the car was legally in the country, following which I promptly received a Purchase Tax invoice for

£400, which my parents helped me pay. Robert really was being as awkward as he could about everything.

At last, the date for my divorce hearing arrived, and I attended court in anticipation of hearing that I would be granted a decree nisi. However, I was shocked when just as my case was about to be heard, Robert's representative solicitor stood up and said that there was a problem with the matter, and requested that the case be adjourned. I was stunned by this occurrence. Following this upset, my solicitor advised that, due to the complexity of Jersey law, we should seek the services of a barrister, which is exactly what we did. On visiting the barrister in his chambers, based in Bodmin, he told me that he thought my husband sounded like 'J R from Dallas'! I had no idea who or what he was referring to but later discovered that it was a saga on television about a dysfunctional, wealthy, feuding American family.

When I relayed this to my parents, we began to watch the programme each week, and I soon realised how he had come to make this remark as Robert bore many of the same characteristics as 'JR'!

After a protracted legal battle, I was finally granted a 'decree nisi' at Exeter Crown Court in August 1978. However, because of Robert's complicated finances, albeit having turned up at the hearing in his Porches whilst at the same time pleading 'poverty', the Judge made a ruling that a three-day hearing be set aside at Winchester Crown Court in November for a financial settlement to be agreed between both parties. The day before I was due to attend the hearing with my solicitor, he rang to say that an offer had been made by Robert's advocates. The settlement was to include all my not insubstantial legal fees being paid in full, and although the marriage had only been of a short duration, a reasonable financial package was also settled. In addition, I would continue to keep the VW Golf. On my solicitor's recommendation, I agreed to this and also accepted that I would completely sever any further claim on Robert. This particularly unhappy chapter of my life was finally over.

I was delighted that I could put the past behind me but totally unprepared for what lay ahead. Just three months later, my father passed away. He had been suffering with kidney trouble, and on a bitterly cold and snowy day in February, he finally succumbed to his illness. This was a great shock to me, and I felt guilty at the pain and anger I had caused him with my behaviour a few years earlier. Now, I could not believe that my father, who was ever the gentleman and had really been such a kind and gentle soul, was gone.

After 27 years of marriage, my mother was devastated at this loss. She had depended on him so much. The evening before my father's funeral, I was comforting my mother and made a rash statement to her. She was crying bitterly and saying, "I can't be on my own". I hugged her and told her I would never leave her. I was to regret those words for evermore.

With the loss of Bill, my mother became anxious about finding work to support herself. My parents had had a very modest lifestyle and, upon my return from Jersey, I had persuaded them to move from their small terraced house to a bungalow. I had helped them with their mortgage which, following my father's death, I paid off with the monies I had received from my divorce settlement. This was to ensure that my mother would have no financial worry. She was in receipt of Widow's benefit and, with my monthly financial support, I told my mother that it was not necessary for her to go out to work. I felt a strong sense of protection towards her, and perhaps looking back, I was my own worst enemy!

The summer following my father's death, my mother and I took a holiday together to the Cotswolds.

I had never visited this area before but immediately felt a familiarity. I fell in love with the honey-coloured houses nestled in the beautiful countryside.

We stayed in a lovely guest house in the small village of Bampton, and it was here that I first met John, my next husband. He was staying at the same guest house with a group of doctors who were visiting from Japan. John was doing research work with them through the University of Kent, where he was a Senior Lecturer.

The first time I saw John, I thought he was someone who was full of nervous energy. He was tall and slim with dark hair and laughing hazel eyes behind metal-trimmed glasses. He had a lovely smile but a shy disposition.

We immediately sensed an attraction between us. One evening, my mother, John, and I, along with the Japanese doctors, enjoyed a drink in a nearby pub. It was a lovely evening and I felt very comfortable in John's presence. Before leaving Bampton, we exchanged addresses. John lived in Canterbury, a place I had never visited, I recall how he was very enthusiastic about the city. On my return home, I wrote to him but did not hear anything until my birthday in December. He rang from his parents' house in Swansea. I felt that John was slightly nervous in his conversation with me and put this down to his shyness. We continued to write to one another, and in one of his letters he revealed that he was married, but was in the midst of trying to agree a separation from his wife. There were no children involved, but the difficulty lay in the fact that his wife not willing to divorce. John asked if he could visit me and, when I told my mother, she agreed that he could stay with us for the weekend, about which I was very happy.

I chose not to tell my mother at this stage that John was married but seeking a divorce. I knew she would not approve. My desire to have a relationship with John was strong enough to make me protective of us both. As I already knew that my mother would be critical of any bond I formed with a member of the opposite sex following my divorce from Robert, I felt I had to use the art of self-preservation!

John paid what was to be the first of many visits in February 1980.

Chapter 8

Laughter and Tears

Initially, my mother was very accommodating when John came to visit me, which was usually every other weekend. She always made him feel very welcome and produced some lovely meals for us all. John and I would go to a dinner dance at the nearby Commodore Hotel in Instow on a Saturday evening, often finishing with a stroll along the nearby beach, which added to a romantic feeling. Very often, I found our weekend's enjoyment marred by Barbara, who would insist on accompanying us for a lunch at a hotel or pub before John would leave to return to his work in Canterbury.

This meant that quality time as a courting couple was hindered by Barbara's presence, which annoyed me intensely, but I could not bring myself to tell my mother that John and I desired some privacy. Also, because I shared my mother's twin bedded room, she was aware of any time I spent with John, which made me very self-conscious.

One day, out of the blue, my mother said, "Well, have you told him that you are adopted?". I told her that I had, and she immediately wanted to know what John's reaction was. I felt that this was an unnecessary intrusion on my personal life. I told her that John was surprised but did not delve into the circumstances behind my adoption. Looking back, she often asked questions like this whenever I struck up a friendship with anyone, be it boy or girl. I think she felt that I was obliged to tell people of my adoption as she considered this a 'badge of honour' in her life. Sadly, once I finally revealed that John was in the process of going through an agreed divorce from his wife, my mother's attitude towards him changed radically. She began to goad me about being involved with a married man, despite the fact that I protested that there were no children involved. Her derisory remarks about us made me more sensitive, especially when she challenged me about the age difference between John and me. He was fourteen years older than me. I told her that, despite her attitude, once the divorce was final, we would get married, whatever her feelings were about the matter.

As John and I made arrangements for our wedding, we decided to buy a house in Canterbury, which would be close to his work at the University. John would live there until I joined him.

I was still working at Shapland and Petter and decided to leave in December 1981 in order to find work in Canterbury. My mother was masterful in cajoling me to invite her to join me when I moved there. She said if she were with John and me, it would keep things 'respectable' whilst we remained unmarried.!

I found a secretarial position at the Registry of the University. This was great because it meant John and I could travel to and from work together. At first, my mother was very enthusiastic about helping us to settle into our new home. She was very helpful cooking, cleaning and even helping with the decorating whilst we were at work. She was a dab hand too, at clearing the overgrown gardens.

Each weekend, John and I found ourselves feeling guilty if we did not include my mother in various shopping trips, visits to National Trust properties or other places of interest. On one occasion, John was planning to take me to the opera at Glyndebourne. My mother's reaction when she heard this was one of incensed jealousy. She started shouting at us, saying, "You don't mind leaving me in the house all week, and now you're going off to enjoy yourselves. I think the very least you can do is to take me as well." This made John very uncomfortable and, in order to placate her, he arranged to take her with us. Glyndebourne was a splendid affair. My mother and I dressed in our finery and enjoyed a lovely picnic in the grounds along with the traditional drink of Pimms. My mother was in her element, especially when she came face to face with Ted Heath, the former Prime Minister. There was a definite hint of snobbery about her as she walked around the grounds. John took great pleasure in introducing me to opera, something I had never experienced before. I have some wonderful memories of our time together, especially when we managed to go on our own. Sadly, such times like these were not to last.

As time went by, my mother started to exert a sense of control over me again. She also attempted to do likewise with John. However, he refused to accept this behaviour from her, and eventually, it led to a breakdown in my relationship with him. I was pulled between the two most important people in my life and didn't want to hurt either of them.

Things reached a pitch at the end of May when, with a broken heart, I reluctantly returned to Bideford with my mother. Sensing that perhaps my relationship with John was over, I felt a tremendous anger within myself at her.

I tried to tell her she was to blame for the break-up between John and me, but she was insensitive to my feelings.

I was deeply hurt by my mother's attitude towards me. One minute she was overly enthusiastic about the wedding, and next, she would say things like, "You've already been married and look how that ended. That should be enough for you." Whenever I tried to retaliate against her, she would begin taunting me about my adoption. She would say, "After all Bill and I have done for you. You are a wicked, ungrateful girl."

I found myself regretting the words I had spoken when my father passed away, that I would never leave her. I began to think that, maybe after all, my place in life was to remain at her side. Guilt is a powerful thing, and this was a hold my mother had over me.

John proved to be my knight in shining armour; he refused to accept that our relationship was over.

He travelled down to see me and, because of the strained atmosphere with Barbara, booked into a local hotel. I joined him for a meal in the evening, and afterwards, we went and confronted my mother, telling her that we were going to get married and she could either be happy for us or stay out of our lives; it was her choice. She capitulated and became positively gushing, telling John that she liked him very much and was only too happy at the thought of him becoming her son-in-law.

On a beautiful sunny day in September 1983, John and I were married. It was a memorable day with members of both sides of our family present. When we set off on our honeymoon, my mother pulled me aside and said I was to go and have a lovely time and not to worry about her, not to even think of ringing her. Was this a veiled hint? Was she making a point that she would be lonely?

Our honeymoon in Switzerland was a very happy time. At last, I felt that I could truly be myself, unfettered by my mother's constant company. As the honeymoon drew to an end, I began to feel a certain unease as we returned home to continue living under the same roof as my mother. We had sold our house in Canterbury because John was moving to the University of Exeter.

My mother's bungalow had only two bedrooms. This meant that any form of newly married privacy was compromised!

It was not long before, once again, my mother began to present herself as an interfering and jealous person. She began putting a lot of pressure on John and me. Her quest to become a grandmother was very evident in her caustic remarks about starting a family.

John and I had a brief respite from her criticism and interference when we took a trip to see his parents in Swansea. Being completely free from pressure, I strongly believe that whilst we were there, I conceived our child.

As Christmas approached, my mother continued making nasty remarks to me about John, saying that she felt I had made a mistake in marrying him. I was already feeling very tense about our restrained life living with her and bellowed at her that it was about time she left us alone. I then added that I thought I could be pregnant.

It was like a bomb had dropped. For once, she stayed quiet.

Having confirmed that I was expecting a baby, John said that maybe this was the time to look into my birth family history, but I was not ready to do this. I knew deep down that if my mother got wind of this she would take it as a snub against her and Bill, so we agreed to let the subject drop.

My mother was very excited at the prospect of her first grandchild and that it would be born in the same month as her birthday, July.

Because of John's transfer to Exeter University, my mother seized upon the chance of ensuring that she would not be left living on her own. She suggested that we all invest in a property together and that she had found the perfect place. She said there was a Bed and Breakfast business for sale with a granny annexe. We were cautious about the suggestion but, knowing that she would be occupying the granny annexe, we agreed to purchase it with her.

We moved into the property at Westward Ho! in April 1984. It was a large semi-detached Victorian property with lovely large rooms and lots of character. It seemed an ideal solution for all of us. However, almost immediately, my mother began her manipulative ways again. She suddenly announced that she intended to let the granny annexe and live within the house so that she could do Bed and Breakfast. John and I were speechless. This was not what we had planned, and no amount of disagreement would change my mother's mind. The atmosphere between us was icy, to say the least. While John was at work, my mother would be quite hostile towards me, saying that I was not supporting her about letting the annexe. I refused to take her side on this issue.

Such was the ill-feeling between John and my mother that he suggested he should leave and that things weren't working out between us all. I was taken back by his words and said, knowing my history, how could he abandon his unborn child and me? We looked at each other in despair and then hugged and kissed. Neither of us wanted to be apart and we were not going to allow my mother to drive a wedge between us.

Sadly, the situation led to life with my mother becoming more strained, especially when John was not working at the university and staying at home. As my pregnancy progressed, my mother began to be more considerate of my well being but I started to feel as though I was being suffocated and could not lead my own life. My mother was so clingy she even suggested that she could be with me at the birth instead of John.

How was I ever going to understand her?

During the course of my pregnancy, I often found myself thinking about my birth mother and wondering how she felt when she was expecting me. Did she have a smooth pregnancy? Was she happy at the prospect of having a baby? How would she feel if she knew that she was going to be a grandmother? So many questions in my head but no way of finding any answers. I began to feel more aware of my adoption and what it really meant when, each time I attended the mother and baby clinic, I was asked questions about my family history that I could not answer. This brought home the fact that being abandoned leaves you with a never-ending feeling of loneliness with no family background to relate to.

Despite the difficulties with my mother, I really enjoyed my pregnancy. I felt excited but also apprehensive. My mother was excited too about the impending birth of her grandchild. Such was her enthusiasm that she became a prolific knitter of baby clothes.

Sometimes I would find myself patting my ever-expanding bump and would often talk to 'him'. I had a strong feeling that I was expecting a boy. My mother was rather disdainful when I mentioned this to her and said, "We prefer girls in our family." I made no response, but hoped in my heart that John and I would be blessed with a son.

John was away when I had my first contractions. I was taken to hospital by ambulance, leaving my mother to ring him. He uttered words of surprise at the news, as the due date for the baby's arrival was not for another couple of weeks. My mother took umbrage and immediately put the phone down on him. She was not impressed. Once in hospital, my contractions ceased. It seemed I was not about to give birth on Friday the 13th after all!

Sunday 15th July 1984 was a glorious sunny day. I rang my mother whilst in labour to let her know how things were going. I immediately sensed by her voice that she was jealous because John was by my side instead of her. My excitement at the forthcoming birth was suddenly shrouded with a sense of guilt, and I regretted having called her. At 9.15 that same evening, I gave birth to William, a beautiful, healthy baby.

John and I were ecstatic. I remember feeling over the moon and having a strong sense of euphoria at the birth of this little being that was truly a part of me. He was flesh of my flesh and blood of my blood. It was like the very best things in life had come together all at once. John rang Barbara to give her the good news. She was happy to hear from him and pleased that all had gone well.

John brought Barbara into the hospital the following day. Her first words on seeing her grandson and me were, "You didn't have a girl, then." I felt dejected; the elation of presenting her with her first grandchild had been squashed. I also saw John's look of disapproval and hurt at her remark. When my aunties arrived to see the baby, my mother was positively glowing about her grandson. All talk of 'girls' had been forgotten.

A week later, John fetched William and me home. My mother made a great fuss of all of us, and so we settled into parenthood.

As the weeks went by, my mother began once again to be critical of any actions John and I took concerning the baby's welfare.

By March of the following year, despite some happy times spent with William, who was the centre of attention, Barbara continued to make derisory comments. She began displaying erratic behaviour and constantly interfered in our lives. She was particularly unkind towards John, making derogatory remarks. One evening when John returned home, she told him he could get the evening meal. John looked bewildered and I hastily said we could send for a take-away, but the episode left us feeling uncomfortable. Life became really difficult for us; it was like walking on eggshells with her.

Barbara clearly adored William. It was almost as if she regarded him as her baby. I tried to be understanding and did not want to hurt her feelings, knowing that she had never been able to have children herself.

One day in April, I had just given William his bath and whilst negotiating the stairs, I fell with him in my arms. My mother immediately rescued him from me, but I was left lying on the stairs, unable to move.

I was in terrible pain and William was crying uncontrollably, which added to the trauma. My mother called an ambulance. Thankfully William was alright, apart from being shaken by everything that was going on. The pain in my back was so bad I needed oxygen and was admitted to hospital, where I was later diagnosed with minor spinal fractures. Armed with painkillers, I was allowed home after a couple of days. On my return home, I was quite emotional. I had missed William and was really glad to have him back in my arms. John made a cup of tea and, unbelievably, the handle of the cup broke sending scalding tea all over my legs. I screamed in pain and shock, which brought Barbara rushing into the sitting room. She shouted at John, telling him to "Get out and leave us alone". A statement which I was later to discover he had taken quite literally.

Later that evening, John went to bed in the adjoining bedroom in order not to cause me any discomfort. We were both in shock at the recent event and said very little to each other.

The following morning he left for work, or so I thought. Apart from saying goodbye, he said nothing to me when he left the house. When I asked my mother to get something from our wardrobe, she discovered that John had taken all his belongings. My mother had finally ousted John from the family home.

Chapter 9

Re-adjustment

After discovering that John had indeed left me, I had an overwhelming sense of desertion. William was less than a year old, and now he too, had been abandoned. It was like history repeating itself!

My mother seemed oblivious to the impact this turn of events had on me. She took a perverse sense of enjoyment by telling anyone we knew, that my husband had left me. She would say, "How could a man leave his sick wife and baby son like that?". She would then add that she was disgusted.

A few days following John's departure, he rang to say he was in the area and could he come to see William. I told him I was quite happy for him to come. Before ending the phone call, he added that his mother would be coming too! When I told Barbara, she was outraged; her eyes glared at me as she said, "Well, you'd better stop them from coming". I stood my ground and refused to take notice of her. When John arrived with his mother, you could cut the atmosphere with a knife. There was an uncomfortable awkwardness between everyone. It was difficult to say anything that would improve the situation. John and I barely had any conversation as both our mothers vied for William's attention. I was hoping that John would suggest that he return to us, but this was not the case. After they left, my mother asked me how I felt about everything. I told her quite bluntly that I was feeling depressed and wished that John would return home. This was not what she wanted to hear. She turned and walked away from me, muttering under her breath.

As I slowly recovered from my accident, I felt that Barbara enjoyed the fact that I was dependent on her for the time being. She knew that I needed her to care for William. When my mother's youngest brother, Malcolm, and his wife Angela came to visit, he told her a few home truths. He told her that the rest of the family were disgusted by her behaviour. He said they blamed her for causing the break-up between John and me. He went on to say that as a result of this, the rest of the family did not wish to associate with us. We had basically been ostracised.

My mother, who had always had a soft spot for her baby brother, was upset that he could speak to her like this, but she remained stubbornly oblivious to his words.

A few weeks after John's visit, I received a letter postmarked Swansea. It was a letter from a solicitor whom he had instructed. The letter said that John was seeking a legal separation and wished for the family home to be placed on the market. His intention was to return to Canterbury to his former employment at the University of Kent and purchase a property there.

I was deeply hurt by the letter and felt that John had readily accepted that our marriage was over. It felt like we were on a one-track route to divorce. I couldn't believe that everything had changed so drastically. I kept asking myself why I was not strong enough to fight my corner for William and me. Part of me wanted desperately to run to John and tell him that I had made a mistake and wanted to be with him. However, I only had to look at my mother and, because of my adoption, a huge sense of guilt flooded through me, and I felt compelled to stay with her. She talked about how I had been abandoned and that she could not believe that it was happening to William. She did not, however, make any suggestion that I try to rebuild my marriage. One day, she suddenly said, "Ah well, we shall have to be known as the 'Merry Widow and the Gay Divorcee'," and started laughing. I felt saddened and hurt by her flippant manner.

By autumn of that same year, following the sale of the house, we moved to a dormer bungalow in the little village of Bucks Cross, a few miles outside Bideford.

Having been ostracised by much of the family, everything seemed very surreal. But my cousin Georgina, who I had always been close to, kept in touch. She would often write or send a little parcel for William, just to let me know she was there for me.

As the months passed, my mother, William, and I would pay regular visits to her brother, Malcolm and his family in Cornwall. On one such occasion, Malcolm's wife, Angela, gave William a cup, plate, and saucer with the name 'Liam' on it. She said that in future, she would call him by this name as it was the Irish derivative of William.

The name has stuck to this day.

Georgina, who worked for the BBC and lived in London, came down to visit her mother and, in turn, came to see us. During the course of one of her visits, she asked me if I had ever felt like tracing my birth family, and if so, she would love to help. I said I had often thought about it but could not see myself doing it very easily whilst living under the same roof as Barbara. Georgina, who had a fascination for family history, was eager to help me discover my roots, and she rekindled in me a long held desire to explore my past. I told her I knew my birth surname but that was all. She said to leave it with her and she would see what she could discover.

Life at our home in Bucks Cross was quite different from what I initially expected. One thing I had not bargained for was John's solicitor implying that I was more than capable of going to work, as my mother could look after my son. I was very hurt by this statement, but as finances were tight and there would be no settlement for Liam until our divorce was finalised, I felt compelled to look for employment. I was deeply upset by John's insensitivity towards me. He knew that by going to work, I would almost certainly miss out on certain milestones in Liam's early childhood, just as he would. John and I finally divorced in 1987.

I was fortunate to return to work at Shapland & Petter in Barnstaple, where I was offered a position as secretary to the Managing Director. The job itself was fantastic but proved to be a great strain because of the fact that each day I would make a round trip to work of over 30 miles, a journey that often took half an hour or more each way. However, one summer evening, I found myself sitting in an endless traffic jam on the Instow road on my journey home. There was no way of contacting my mother to let her know that I was delayed. In my frustration, I cried bitterly as I sat in the car. I was so upset at the thought of being so near and yet so far from my darling son. The whole experience made me feel very lonely, abandoned and hurt at how things had turned out. That evening was a deciding factor to look for a job closer to home. Some months later, I found a position at an Independent Boys' Boarding School (Grenville College) working as secretary to the Bursar. It was a challenging but enjoyable job. As I would watch the boys lining up for assembly or running to their classes, with the masters wearing their flowing gowns and caps on their heads, I was reminded of the film, 'Goodbye Mr.Chips'. The school had such a great atmosphere of times gone by, and I loved every aspect of it. After Liam left Junior school, he joined the College, and when he reached Sixth Form, he was made Head Boy. It was a very proud day for his Nan and me. John, too, was delighted by his achievements.

In the early days of my work at Grenville, when Liam was tiny, I was invited to go on a free train trip via the travel agents with whom I booked air and train tickets. The trip was to London, and I was delighted at the thought of an 'away day'. My thoughts went to John. I rang him at his office to see if he would like to meet up for a few hours, and he jumped at the chance. I felt excited at the thought of seeing John but knew that I could not tell my mother of our meeting as, given past experiences, I was afraid of her reaction.

Having met me at Paddington Station, John and I were happy to be in each other's company again. We spent a lovely few hours together and, as we travelled back to the station by taxi, John asked if I would consider getting back together. My heart wanted to say 'yes', but my mind was filled with guilt over my mother. Once again, I failed myself in following my true feelings.

John continued to visit Liam on a regular basis, initially coming to the house where my mother would sometimes be hospitable but on other occasions quite rude and unkind. I began to find John's visits a strain, especially after our brief time together in London. I knew deep down that I still had feelings for him and respected him as Liam's father. Because things remained awkward at home, I began to take Liam out to meet John in Bideford. We would spend time in the park and go to a cafe for a drink, spending a couple of hours with John before he left to return home. After each visit, I would find myself feeling torn with guilt. John was so loyal to Liam, making such a long journey to see him every couple of weeks.

One day in January 1992, during a visit by John, he suddenly announced that he had just re-married and was on his way to tell his parents. I was sitting in the car with him and Liam at the time and felt quite sick at what he had told me. He said he had not yet told his parents about his marriage because it was 'complicated'. He went on to say that his wife had three children and that he would be moving to Ramsgate to live in her home. I asked him, "How could you marry someone with three children when you couldn't stay in a marriage with me and your only son?" He replied, "I didn't really want us to divorce, but I had to divorce your mother." What could I say?

When I told Barbara about John's news, she was gobsmacked and her attitude towards him became more venomous.

As Liam grew older, he would go out with John on his own. On such occasions, Liam would return home laden with toys. One day, when Liam got out of the car with a particularly large carrier bag, I told John that I objected to him spending his money so wastefully and that it would be better to put it in a savings account for Liam. He told me it was up to him what he did for Liam and, as I turned to walk away, he shouted at me, saying, "Make the most of him, Krystyna, because you won't have him much longer". He added that he was applying for custody of Liam. I was speechless and could find no words to respond. In my heart, I was convinced that this could only have come about because John's new wife had cajoled him into it. I spent several anxious weeks watching the post. A letter finally arrived with a date for the hearing, but I was staggered to read that the hearing would be in Canterbury. This meant that I had to take time off work and travel to Kent. As Liam was at school, my mother would have to remain home to look after him. She would like to have come with me as support, but I told her not to worry as I would have support from Liam's godmother, Irene. Irene and I had been friends since we met when working at the University of Kent.

On the day of the hearing, Irene accompanied me to the court. As I sat nervously waiting to go into the hearing, I was suddenly confronted by John's wife. She came over to introduce herself to me and said, "We are doing this for Liam's sake." I was so anxious and overcome with emotion that I collapsed and had to be taken to a side room to compose myself.

Later, in the courtroom, where John's wife was insistent she should be present too, I was relieved when the Judge told her she was not involved in the matter. Despite her protestations, she was escorted by the Clerk of the Court out of the room. A few minutes later, the Judge dismissed the case saying that, as the mother and child concerned resided in North Devon, the matter should be heard in Barnstaple, not Canterbury, and he added that he would be recommending that a report be prepared by Social Services. I suddenly found myself seething with contempt at John for putting his son and me through what I felt would be a gruelling ordeal.

The outcome of this situation made my mother even more hostile towards John. Following this ordeal, whenever John rang to speak to Liam, my mother would hover over him and say in a loud voice that John was a 'nasty man'. She would also try to encourage Liam to tell John to stay away. This tense period of time took its toll on Liam, who later became quite poorly and was off school for several weeks. The Welfare Officer duly visited our home and chatted to Liam. He also talked to me and to my mother, who was only too ready to tell him that she and my father had adopted me. I could see by the man's face that he was not really interested, but he had no option but to listen. I felt embarrassed and wished I could crawl away. Following everyone involved being spoken to, it was then a case of waiting for the outcome of the Welfare Officer's report. Finally, his recommendation revealed that Liam should continue to maintain contact with John but that any visits were to take place only in Liam's home town.

When Liam reached his teenage years, his relationship with John began to mellow and became stronger as the years passed. I was grateful for this, as deep down, I always knew that John was a good man and had an unrelenting love for Liam. This re-adjustment to my life was something I would never wish to repeat. It was a period that had been filled with much angst and remorse.

Chapter 10

Love's Escape

As the years passed, Liam and I shared many happy times with Barbara, especially when we went on holidays. These were often spent in the Cotswolds, which became a firm favourite for all of us. We also visited some relations who had remained friendly towards us. After several years of enduring a fractured relationship with the majority of Barbara's family, a degree of friendship had been reborn. Sadly, we had missed out on several family weddings and christenings; despite Barbara's brother, Malcolm begging her to attend sibling funerals, she had chosen to remain aloof, about which Liam and I felt very uncomfortable.

Liam's school career culminated in him gaining a place at the University of Warwick, where he read Film and Television. In the summer of 2005, he graduated on his twenty-first birthday. It was a memorable and poignant occasion when we celebrated this double event with Liam's friends and family. I was pleased that, along with Barbara and Liam's godmother, Irene, John also joined us. It was a proud moment as John and I sat together watching Liam receive his degree. John and I agreed that we had both made a mistake when we divorced, but we would always remain the best of friends, knowing that we would always love and value our wonderful son.

During the course of my working life, I did experience some short-term relationships with a boyfriend but, as soon as any serious friendship threatened, my mother would start to apply a cunning psychological pressure on me, which inevitably resulted in the relationship ending. I began to live a life of quiet resignation. I imagined that I would remain on my own forever and that a relationship would never be achieved whilst my mother was alive. It was obvious that Barbara felt my place in life was to remain the ever dutiful daughter!

One day, during a conversation, I said to Barbara that I wished I could find someone to share my life with, to which she responded, "What about me? You could leave me on my own, could you? How can you be so selfish, after all Bill and I have done for you over the years?" This hurt me and made me once again feel guilty. At the same time, I longed to be 'free' to lead my life. I began wishing that I had never been adopted. I had lived with the constant reminder that I had been 'chosen' and it felt like a noose around my neck. As much as I appreciated all that my parents had done for me, I found it both a scourge and a blessing.

However, all was not lost for me. Things took on a different perspective when a particularly ardent admirer refused to accept my excuses for ignoring his advances! Jeff, who was also employed at the College as supervisor on the maintenance team, often came to my rescue when I had an emergency at home, such as the washing machine breaking down or the shower unit not working. My mother was always very relieved and grateful to him for his help. One evening Jeff arrived at the house on his motorbike. My mother was very excited at seeing the bike and regaled Jeff with stories of her exploits in the ATS during the war. She was full of enthusiasm as she told him about having rides on motorbikes from the American soldiers based near her camp.

Jeff was married at this time, and this was a reason why I would not entertain his advances. However, it became apparent that all was not happy in his marriage and one day, he announced that he and his wife were getting divorced.

Following the divorce, Jeff continued to try and win me over, constantly asking me to go out with him and, eventually, I gave in. I had always admired Jeff and was attracted by his personality, good looks, and lovely smile that lit up his grey-blue eyes. His hair gave him a touch of the 'silver fox'. We began going out for a drink or meal but, once my mother realised that I was going out with Jeff on a regular basis, she started to show her usual pattern of control. She would interfere with arrangements Jeff and I had made, suddenly announcing that she wanted to go out for a meal, thus throwing our own plans into disarray. As she began to be more awkward about my relationship with Jeff, I had no alternative but to be furtive about where I was going and what I was doing. I could not cope with her snide remarks about Jeff, but I also did not want to incur her wrath. It was a case of trying to maintain a quiet life.

Eventually, however, I was caught out in my clandestine romance. One weekend, I had arranged to go on a 'fictitious' course on behalf of the College, which meant staying away overnight. However, a call from a member of staff asking for me meant that my mother realised I was not where I had said I was! I had been rumbled.

Unaware of the call, I arrived home to find my mother in one of her moods, not realising the cause of it. She asked me if I had enjoyed my time away. I said I had and, as I was about to drink a cup of tea, she said, "Now, tell me the truth, where have you really been?" I was stunned. I swallowed deeply then replied that I had been with Jeff and stayed overnight with him. I then told her that Jeff had proposed to me and that we were now engaged.

This brought a positively explosive reaction from her. She was absolutely incensed that I could even think of marrying a 'workman'! I showed her my engagement ring, but she waved her hand at me and said, "I don't wish to know." The hours following this revelation were filled with an intense atmosphere of discomfort. Even the dog was shaking with fear as my mother raged as she went around the house. Later that night, I rang Liam and told him everything that had passed between Barbara and me. Whilst he was happy about my engagement, he was worried about his Nan's attitude to the news. He knew only too well how nasty she could be when things were not as she liked.

My mother's acidic remarks about Jeff meant that day-to-day life was far from happy. She continually tried to wear me down, telling me that she would do everything possible to prevent me marrying Jeff. When it was bedtime, she would suddenly throw open my bedroom door and start shouting at me, saying, "You are an ungrateful daughter. Mark my words, you'll be sorry one day for what you are doing to me."

I suddenly found everything very hard to cope with, and it even started to affect my work through lack of concentration and the turmoil that was going on in my head. I was astounded when, one evening, she told me to give her my front door key and said that I would have to ring the doorbell in future to come back in. Afraid of her reaction, I gave in and handed it to her. I never saw the key again! I felt like a child, having to knock on the door each time I needed to get in the house. I was so embarrassed I did not tell Liam or anyone else. It was unbelievable that this was how things had developed. Because of the pressure that Barbara was putting on me, I very nearly gave in and thought of telling Jeff that we could not marry; however, Liam was so supportive whenever we managed a phone call, often when at work or on the way home. I did not dare to speak to him in front of my mother. I rang John to tell him what had transpired, and he too was supportive and wished Jeff and me well. He said he believed my mother was jealous of me and could not bear the thought of me having any form of happiness in life with a partner. He added that he believed Barbara was, in effect, abusing me and had done so throughout my life. This revelation shocked me. I had never looked at my mother's behaviour in this way and it felt like a 'wake-up' call.

Sadly, amidst this turmoil, we received the news that Uncle Malcolm's wife, Angela, had died. We were very upset as, over the years, we had shared some very happy times with her and her little Jack Russell, Soda, whom Liam loved playing with. In early November, on a foggy day, we travelled to her funeral in Cornwall. As I was getting into the car, my mother told me to remove my engagement ring. She said that she did not want any of her family to know that I was getting married. I was hurt by her comment, but her glaring eyes said enough, and I capitulated. However, remembering what John had recently said to me, I suddenly felt indignant at her control of me. I placed the engagement ring back on my finger but added an additional one just to placate her. She had, in a way, won again!

Later that day, when we were all gathered at the wake, Liam encouraged me to tell some of the family about my impending wedding and how Barbara was being so nasty about it. They were shocked about her behaviour and told me that she had no right to dictate my life. Malcolm said that despite Barbara being his sister, whom he loved dearly, she was a 'naughty girl'. An echo of the remark my grandmother had made many years ago. With members of the family showing their support and Liam telling me I should listen to them, I began to gain a sense of confidence.

However, despite this, I still found myself fearful enough to sneak personal belongings from the house in preparation for my marriage. My mother's resigned but cold attitude towards my impending wedding made things extremely awkward and uncomfortable. I would surreptitiously take little bits and pieces out each morning as I went to work and pass them to Jeff for safe-keeping. It sounds strange now, but basically, I was terrified of what my mother might do given her volatile behaviour. I was, without doubt, afraid of her. Liam continued to show his support as he tried to persuade his Nan to see things from my point of view. He told her that he fully approved of Jeff and me getting married. He also told her that he thought Jeff was a very nice, caring person and that she should be happy for me. She was scornful of Liam's remarks and, in turn, gave us both a hard time. This made the atmosphere in the house awkward and uncomfortable for us all whenever Liam was home. I was glad now that Liam was working away in Warwickshire as he did not have to witness everything that went on between Barbara and me. Unfortunately, despite his support, he would not be able to attend our wedding because of prior commitments but assured me that he would be with us in spirit.

I reminded my mother of the date of our wedding several times, but she remained hostile in any conversation on the subject. However, she was cunning in the manner in which she would lean on me about other matters, which she knew I would not say no to. For all that had transpired over the years of my life, I found this period of time the most difficult and debilitating.

Happiness finally came on a cold but sunny day in late January 2007, when Jeff and I were married at Northam Registry Office. We were supported by one of my mother's brothers, Alfred, his wife, Anna, and Georgina's mother, Ruby. Together with our best man and his wife, we were a very small wedding party indeed.

Needless to say, my mother was conspicuous by her absence!

Chapter 11

Trials and Tribulations

Following my marriage, which had been a quiet affair, Jeff and I enjoyed a simple pub lunch with my uncle, two aunts and our two friends. The following day we took an overnight trip to visit Liam in Leamington Spa. It was good to see him, and we had a celebratory meal together. He was apologetic about not being able to attend our wedding, but Jeff and I both assured him that it was his love and support that was the most important.

A few days later, on my return to work, I telephoned my mother and arranged to meet her for lunch. She was pleasantly receptive towards me on the phone, which was a relief. However, later as she got into my car, her eyes immediately went to my left hand and, seeing my wedding ring said, "You did it then". I chose to ignore her gibe. She made no further comment on the matter, but after lunch, she told me she would expect me for dinner later! She had put me on the spot; how was I to say no? After work, I joined her for the meal but told her that I was not prepared to do this again unless Jeff was included. Needless to say, this remark was met with a vehement refusal. She said, "That man is not coming here, ever." I was very sad that this was her attitude. I had hoped that she would accept Jeff as we were now married.

My mother continued to be very scathing about us to both her family and friends. Liam's godmother, Irene, who frequently rang my mother, told me that she could no longer entertain Barbara's vitriolic manner and would not be ringing her again!

A delicate pattern of life existed between Barbara and me. Each time I saw her, I would breathe a sigh of relief when I left. She reluctantly agreed that things had changed for us both. In reality, Barbara was not a person who could live happily on her own. Whenever the opportunity arose, she would make a point of telling me that she disliked living alone. This left me bearing a continual sense of guilt.

I tried to appease her by taking her out on trips at weekends, even though it prevented Jeff and me having some quality time together. I also took her on a short holiday to the Cotswolds but, rather than rebuilding our mother-daughter relationship, it remained distanced, especially as I had to continue ignoring her innuendo that I should leave Jeff. She simply could not accept that I was married and, consequently, was leading my own life.

Throughout the many years I had shared with Barbara, there had been some very good times. We had both enjoyed shopping trips, and I like to think my appreciation of fashion was because my mother had always had good dress sense. We had many enjoyable holidays whilst Liam was growing up. However, married life had given me a new-found independence, which meant the relationship between my mother and me was now very strained. One could say that when things were good, they were very good, but when they were bad, they were dire!

This turbulent lifestyle changed drastically when, one day in early January 2010, I made my usual morning phone call to my mother. It took some time for her to answer. When she did, I was met by her dog, Tess, barking madly. My mother's weak voice uttered my name as she then said, "I can't get up." I immediately drove to the house only to find that I could not gain entry and had to resort to calling an ambulance and, in turn, the police to help break into the house. Upon entry, we discovered my mother had broken her leg, which meant her being admitted to hospital. As I stayed alongside my mother whilst awaiting her operation, she asked me what I was going to do. I told her that I would help her as much as I could, and would look after Tess in the house if she was happy for me to do so. She responded by asking, "Can I trust you? I don't want 'him' in the house, you know that, don't you?" I answered that Jeff was happy for me to do whatever was necessary. So, with a certain anxiousness, I stayed at Barbara's to look after Tess and the house until her return from hospital. I initially thought this would be for just a week or so but, due to complications, she did not return for several weeks.

Although my mother was still hostile towards me, even in front of the nursing staff, she accepted that she had no one else to rely upon for help. I found it quite a strain travelling to the hospital each day and also trying to get home to Jeff. I did not want him to feel that I had abandoned him to care for my mother. Although he was very supportive, he was concerned for my well-being with everything that was going on. When Barbara was told she could go home, I told her that it would be necessary for both Jeff and me to arrange a bedroom for her downstairs in the dining room, as it was no longer possible for her to get upstairs. She grudgingly gave in to the suggestion and was happy for Jeff to help me. When she arrived home, Jeff briefly wished her well and quickly retreated to our home in Woolsery to avoid any possible confrontation.

Because of Barbara's incapacity and her inability to care for Tess, I felt I had no option but to remain in the house with her. Unbelievably, Tess died within a few days of Barbara's return home. I couldn't believe it, and worse still, my mother refused to believe that Tess had died, even though she was lying stiffly beside her! It took a great deal of diplomacy and a visit from the veterinary nurse to persuade Barbara that Tess had indeed died! This made Barbara very bitter towards me. She blamed me for causing Tess's death. I knew, deep down, that she was grieving, so ignored her angry words. In order to placate her, Jeff made every effort to find another Pomeranian that would give my mother something to focus on. Barbara was really appreciative of his efforts, and more so when he found a replacement dog, which she named Kim. She was delighted to have a companion again. However, there was one drawback. It meant that, as my mother was unable to move about the house easily, it was necessary for me to remain at the house with her so that I could care for both her and the new dog. He was only a year old and had not been house-trained very well! This meant that I had yet another call upon my already busy time.

A few days following Kim's arrival, Barbara suffered the loss of her youngest brother, Malcolm. This was an added blow to her already vulnerable emotions. It was a big shock for us all as Liam and I had been very close to

Malcolm, both as a confidant and a very supportive uncle. Because of Barbara's inability to travel, she was very upset and agitated when she realised she was unable to attend Malcolm's funeral. Also, because of Barbara's incapacity, it meant that Jeff and I too were unable to attend. I found this very hard to accept, as it brought back memories of how I had been precluded from attending my grandmother's funeral when I was sixteen. I was expected to lay out the food in preparation for the wake and had had to remain in the house watching out of the kitchen window as the funeral cortege left. A day I have never forgotten. I had been robbed of the opportunity to pay my respects to a very dear grandmother who had cared for me so often in my childhood.

As the weeks passed, my mother realised it was becoming impossible for me to constantly travel back and fore between her and Jeff. She asked us to come and live with her. We gathered together to discuss the idea, and as we did so, Barbara made overtures to Jeff, saying she had nothing against him and would be only too happy for us both to share her home.

After some consideration, Jeff and I moved from our home in Woolsery and, together with our cat, Simba, moved in with Barbara: a move that family and neighbours frowned upon. They were only too aware of Barbara's challenging ways and did not think it was a good idea.

Life began to take on a reasonable sense of day to day normality. I looked after all of my mother's personal care, as well as all the usual household chores.

In early July, Jeff and I took Barbara on holiday. We had hired a self-catering lodge in Herefordshire. It was a lovely place and, together with Kim, everything was very congenial. Jeff was very attentive towards Barbara, assisting her in and out of the car and taking Kim for walks. I thought that we had turned a corner at last and that my mother had accepted that Jeff was now part of the family.

I was wrong!

Following Liam's departure after a visit one weekend, we had said our good-byes and, as we shut the door, Jeff asked Barbara if she was alright. She suddenly turned on Jeff in a fit of jealous outrage, shouting, "Am I alright, am I alright? No, I am not."

She could not come to terms with Jeff receiving a hug from Liam, even though she had been hugged herself by him. She gave Jeff an unending tirade of verbal abuse, full of hatred, her eyes blazing across the room at me. I looked on in stunned amazement. Jeff, taken by surprise at her wild accusations, retaliated, telling her a few home truths and saying he did not like the way she was treating me as a slave rather than a daughter. This was like a red rag to a bull. She swore at both of us and told us to get out of her house and her life.

A few hours later, Jeff and I had come to the decision that we should return to Woolsery. I told my mother that I was arranging for us to go back to our former home. Her reaction to this was a complete reversal. She said, "I wouldn't be too hasty if I were you. I think you should stay, and we won't make any more of what has been said." Of course, in her cunning way, she knew that she would be unable to cope on her own. Jeff, knowing how torn I would be if I turned my back on my mother, agreed that we would give it another go.

Life for us was now like treading on eggshells. Barbara no longer wished for Jeff to take Kim for his daily walks, which was a disappointment for him as he had grown fond of the little dog. She also curtailed his movements within the house. She became very antagonistic whenever he was nearby. This resulted in Jeff remaining upstairs in our bedroom for most of the time, even when eating his meals. He managed to do a limited amount of gardening, which provided some respite for him. If Jeff and I were out shopping, we were blighted by Barbara ringing to check how long we would be. I felt awful for Jeff being subjected to such an uncomfortable existence. I was also deeply upset at the way our life was being controlled by Barbara but could see no way of easing the stress this was causing. Something had to give, and it did!

One day in early April 2013, Jeff and I were shopping in Morrisons. I had not been feeling well and was suddenly taken ill in the shop. An ambulance was called and, after being admitted to hospital, I was diagnosed as having had a stroke. When Jeff returned home to tell my mother what had happened, she was very upset and concerned for me.

My absence from home resulted in Barbara becoming wholly reliant on Jeff! Surprisingly, she allowed him to assist her in her day to day care, providing all meals and personal help. I returned home a few days later to find my mother positively glowing in her admiration of Jeff. Fortunately, the effects of my stroke were not life changing but I was now on medication and still had to undergo further tests. I had also been advised to rest as much as possible. This meant Jeff suddenly found himself looking after both his mother-in-law and me!

Barbara realised that things would have to change due to my health issues and her own inability to help. She decided to arrange some 'home help' which, as it turned out, proved to be very minimal, just hoovering and dusting! There was no personal care, so Jeff and I continued to do this for Barbara.

As my strength recovered, I found myself returning to much of what I had been doing prior to my stroke. My mother sadly reverted to her usual pattern of paranoia.

Incredibly, despite all that Jeff had done for her, he found himself once more confined to our bedroom. Barbara would accuse him of eavesdropping or lurking with some intent. Throughout her tirade of abuse, Jeff remained tolerant for my sake.

Whenever relations visited, they were appalled by Barbara's insensitivity towards Jeff, but they did not challenge her, as they knew only too well that she could turn on them too. There was no easy way out of our situation, so life became a matter of 'grin and bear it'.

One evening, my mother and I were watching the television programme Long Lost Family, a series tracing lost family members. She turned to me and asked if I ever felt like trying to find my real family. I told her I had often wondered about them but would not wish to upset her, to which Barbara said, "I wouldn't bother if I were you. You might not like what you find." I was sorry that this was her reaction. I had hoped she would open up to me and at last tell me what she knew. Once again, I thought I would never discover who I really was, but a chink of light was to come from my cousin, Georgina. She had always been fascinated that I was adopted and longed for me to try and discover my roots. When she visited one day, we secretly arranged that she would make contact with North Devon Social Services on my behalf. She rang me a few days later to say that she had arranged for us to visit in the hope of gaining access to my adoption papers.

On the pretext of a hospital appointment, I arranged to meet Georgina to visit the Social Services office in Barnstaple. I was very apprehensive and Georgina, sensing my nervousness, asked me if I was sure that I wanted to do this. She was concerned that I should not feel under any pressure by her. I told her this was something I had wanted to do for a very long time and that, with her support, I was more than ready to do so.

A very friendly lady approached us as we entered the offices. She introduced herself and took us into a small, windowless room. She chatted to me at length about my desire to see my papers. Satisfied that I was quite happy about whatever I would discover, she went to fetch my file. I began to feel a surge of fear. It was like being on the edge of a precipice; I was about to find my true identity. Georgina and I were left to view a rather large file of papers. I had a growing sense of excitement but also a sense of guilt within me. It felt like I was betraying everything Barbara and Bill had done for me. As we viewed the papers, the first thing that became evident was that the surname I had so often searched for was wrong. It was not Franska, as written on my original birth certificate; it should have read Szafranska. Georgina and I looked at each other shocked, and I was overcome with tearful emotion.

I was told I could take my file of papers away, but I could not bring myself to take them home with me because I would have felt guilty. Instead, I entrusted the precious papers to Georgina and gave her my full blessing to research what she could from them.

When I arrived home, I was shaking with excitement. At last, after all these years, I was going to find my true identity. In the meantime, I needed to contain myself because there was no way that I would reveal to my mother what I had done.

Bill, Barbara and Krystyna

Krystyna's adopted family

Krysia and Leslie

Ursula, Sofia (mother), Maria and Krysia

The Szafranska family L - R. Maria, Sofia, Genia, Krysia,
Zosia, Maxymilian & Ursula

Maxymilian, Ursula, Krysia & Maria after
mother's funeral in Tehran

Anthill in Kenya

Ursula, Krysia and Maria in Mombasa

Resettlement Camp near Cirencester

Krysia with Pepe

Ursula, Richard & Krystyna

Alex, Richard, Krystyna & Roger – Family reunited

Chapter 12

Exits and Entrances

Christmas 2015 was a quiet affair. My mother's health was rapidly declining. Thankfully, she had finally made her peace with Jeff, acknowledging that he was indeed a good man. "You're alright," she said one evening as Jeff and I sat by her bedside. Her welcome words of approval had been a long time coming.

Sadly, just as the New Year entered, we received news of the death of Barbara's sister-in-law, Anna. Just six weeks later, this was followed by the death of Alfred, Barbara's last surviving brother, and Anna's husband. This proved to be a double shock for my mother, and I am sure that her health went into further decline following these losses.

I was worried by how long my mother began sleeping each day; it just wasn't like her. She seemed to lose interest in everything going on around her. I made a secretive phone call to my mother's doctor, who also happened to be my doctor. Having voiced my concerns, she began visiting my mother more frequently. Barbara's appetite had all but disappeared, and I noticed too that she was becoming quite thin. One day in early March, following one of the doctor's now regular visits, she warned me that Barbara's demise was not far off and told me that I should warn Liam. As she left, I closed the door feeling numb with shock. Could this really be happening? When I told Liam, he came down the following weekend. Unfortunately, the timing could not be worse as he was already coping with the terminal illness of his father, John. He was now faced with the sight of his nan's failing health. Like me, he could not believe that his nan's life was on the ebb. It was with great reluctance that he left to return home to London.

I, too, found it hard to accept that my mother's death was imminent. The house took on a quiet, peaceful atmosphere. Barbara's decline in health meant that her usual demands were no longer voiced. It was almost alien to me not to hear her persistent call for my attention. Suddenly I found myself wandering about the house feeling lost; I could not settle to anything. Nurses visited daily, more for observation purposes than hands-on care. They would leave smiling at me but saying very little. What was there to say? Life was now a waiting game for the inevitable.

Barbara took her last breath on a sunny afternoon in April 2016. She was 90 years of age. Jeff and I were devastated. Liam and Jane, his fiancee, had driven down earlier that day, and now we all gathered to share our grief. Despite all that he had endured from Barbara, Jeff took on the mantle of informing family members that she had passed away. He was almost as lost as me by the loss of this dominant lady.

Later that same evening, after the funeral director had been, I found Liam standing by his nan's now empty bed. I stole away, silently breaking into tears once more. I could sense his overwhelming loss of his other 'parent', as he had often called his nan.

Although one knows that death is a part of life, I still found myself walking around the house in a stunned daze. I took myself upstairs to my mother's bedroom as if seeking solace. I gazed around the room and my eyes fell upon her jewellery box. For some reason, I was drawn towards it. I lifted the lid, and there lying on top, was an envelope addressed, 'Krystyna and Liam'. I stared at it, then tentatively opened it to find she had written a letter to us. I noted the date, September 1999 - the year Liam and I had gone to visit New York for the first time with Uncle Malcolm, as my mother was not sure about flying that far. As my eyes scanned the first few words, I was overcome with emotion, and with tears coursing down my cheeks, I called Liam. As he entered the room, I held the letter out to him as I shook with emotional anguish. We both read the letter and then stood hugging one another. After all the years of coping with my mother's often erratic behaviour, I had always loved her. And now, here was proof that she had, in her own odd way, always loved me too, and also of course, Liam. I still cannot read that letter without a lump in my throat.

Over the years, my mother, or Mum as I began to call her later in life, had given me various items of jewellery. One piece was a charm for my bracelet. It was of a spider in a web. I remembered how she had said at the time that this was how she viewed me, a spider in a web! In a strange way, she was right. All my life, I had been 'tied' one way or another, unable to ever feel free. Now I was free, and whenever I look at this charm, I am reminded of her words.

I found the days leading up to the funeral incredibly hard to cope with. I missed Mum with an overbearing sorrow. No words can adequately describe just how much.

The once large family, which had numbered ten in total, was now reduced to one remaining sibling, Ruby, Georgina's mother. So, on the day of Mum's funeral, we were a small gathering in the cemetery chapel. When I saw the hearse bearing Mum's coffin, it was almost too much to bear. This to me, was confirmation that she had finally left us.

The days following the funeral found me in a deep melancholy state. Liam and Jane had returned home to London. Jeff was as supportive as he could be under the circumstances, and I know that he, too, missed Mum. I found myself ringing Mum's sister, Ruby, almost every day. There was a similarity in their voices, which was a comfort to me. She was very understanding as I cried uncontrollably down the phone, telling her how much I missed Mum. It was a passage of grieving that was necessary for me to come to terms with her death.

Eventually, I began to acclimatise to the loss and my spirits began to lift. After all, in August we could all look forward to Liam and Jane's wedding! I turned my attention to the fact that I was now a free person, to do whatever I wished to do without having to account for it.

Sadly, as June commenced, death and loss would once again take hold of our family. This time, it was Liam's father, John, who passed away, following a brave fight with cancer over a number of years. His death, coming only six weeks after Liam's nan, was a heavy burden for Liam, and I felt desperately sorry for him. What a year it was turning out to be. Unfortunately, as Jeff and I would be on a planned holiday to Southern Ireland, we were unable to support Liam on the day of John's funeral, something that disappointed me greatly. After all, without John, there would have been no Liam. No matter what had gone on before, Liam would always be a constant reminder of a love lost. Once again, I found it hard to come to terms with yet another loss.

As the weeks went by, we all began to turn our minds to the wedding. This proved to be just what was needed to enliven everyone's spirits. On a late August day, Liam and Jane were married, and what a lovely occasion it turned out to be. As well as being a day of much needed celebration, the occasion brought about a moment of reconciliation with John's family. Since the day that John had left Liam and me, there had been no contact. Now, we were able to put the past behind us and move on.

Although the day was full of happiness, I saw a hint of sadness in Liam's eyes. I knew it was because of the absence of two very special people in his life, his father and his nan.

And so it was that I eventually began to acclimatise to what had been, so far, a year of many sorrows. But now, I could turn to doing things that I wanted to do without feeling guilty.

With my newfound freedom, my mind started to turn to the papers Georgina and I had collected from Social Services more than four years previously. During this time, Georgina had found some possible leads but had nothing firm to base them on. She had found a few references to the name Szafranska, which, we now knew, was my birth mother's correct surname. Georgina had encountered a bit of a conundrum when a second Krystyna Szafranska came to light! This lady was born in 1929, the same year of birth as the first Krystyna. She had been born in Warsaw and was an actress. She died in Rome in 2002. Whilst researching this lady, Georgina discovered that she had known the late Pope John Paul II! During the Second

World War, they had both been involved in a theatre group in Warsaw called Teatr Niegrommy, roughly translated as the Non-Enormous Theatre. Georgina and I both fantasised that my birth might be like the well-known love story, The Thornbirds, by Colleen McCullough. This later became a film series, staring Richard Chamberlain. It told of a forbidden love between a priest and a young woman! Of course, we realised that this idea was too fantastical for words, but we just couldn't believe that, in searching for my birth mother's name, we would come across two people bearing the same name and year of birth. Georgina found a photograph of Krystyna the actress, and Jeff and I, in turn, sent her photos of me in my early twenties just to see if we could see a similarity, but there wasn't. Sense finally prevailed, and Georgina decided to look closer at the Krystyna Szafranska who was recorded as marrying Leslie Corke in March 1957.

However, we were still baffled as there was no record of this particular Krystyna ever giving birth. The search became an almost thankless task. We just could not find any positive proof to connect me to either of the two Krystynas.

After the initial sense of excitement at finding my adoption papers, I now began to feel deeply disappointed. Would I ever discover my roots?

As I sat watching television one evening, the programme Long Lost Family came on. I turned to Jeff and said, "I really feel I would like to join the Ancestry website".

This site had been advertised on several occasions. Jeff said, "What's stopping you?" He was only too happy for me to do whatever I wished, saying that I had been suppressed long enough during my life.

I joined in the late summer of 2016 and decided to go one step further and undertake a DNA test. Georgina was delighted when I told her, but Liam was a little apprehensive, as he did not want me to get hurt by whatever I might discover. Having put his mind at rest, we eagerly awaited the results.

A few weeks later, when the results arrived, I was filled with nervous tension as I cast my eyes over the information and viewed the list of possible matches. Sadly, rather than being excited at the findings, I was confused and rather disappointed. I don't know what I was expecting, but somehow I thought the answer to my many questions would be staring back at me in black and white. They weren't.

With Georgina's help, I made contact with some of the possible matches via the internet, but as the weeks passed, I began to resign myself to the fact that I was not going to be successful in my quest.

My despondency was lifted in March 2017. Jeff and I had gone to visit Georgina and her family in Yorkshire. Whilst there, an e-mail arrived in my Ancestry in-box. It was from someone called Roger, who was living in Rochester, New York. I couldn't believe it; finally, I had had a response! As we started to message one another, it became clear that Roger was a blood cousin as his grandmother was my maternal grandfather's sister!

The elation within me was 'off the scale', and more was to follow.

Chapter 13

A far-reaching tale!

My excitement at receiving contact from a living blood relative was almost too much to comprehend.

I had spent too many years imagining how I would feel if I ever found my birth family, and now I was about to face the reality. I was about to open the door that would reveal how I came to be abandoned. I felt both nervous and excited at the same time. Roger shared what little information he knew about his grandmother, Marianna.

The most important revelation was the surname - Szafranska.

Marianna Szafranska, and her sister, Ludwika, had left their home in Poznań, Poland in 1910 and travelled to the USA, where they eventually found work as housemaids in Rochester, New York. Marianna and her sister had a younger brother, Maxymilian Szafranski, who had remained in Poland. In 1911 Marianna married Ignatius Hurysz. Their son Casimer married Theresa Warchol, and they had three sons, Paul, Roger and Theodore. Their middle son, Roger, married Kathleen Herring, and they went on to have three daughters.

Kathleen, or Kathy as she is known, had a keen interest in genealogy, as a consequence of which she joined Ancestry. Having received some interesting results, Kathy persuaded Roger to do the same and also to take a DNA test. When Roger received his results, he thought they looked 'boring'! They indicated a 100% Eastern European background which, given what he already knew, came as no surprise to him.

It was only later when Kathy started investigating her ancestry and building her own family tree, that Roger looked again at his Ancestry site. To his surprise, he discovered my message of some months ago.

This led to the start of many e-mails between Roger, Georgina and me. I needed to keep Georgina in the loop as she was so much better than me at researching any information that Roger might provide.

Roger's greatest revelation was that one of Maxymilian's daughters, Ursula, was living in Ealing, London, just a short distance from my son, Liam. This meant that Ursula was my blood aunt and Liam's great aunt. I couldn't believe it.

Roger told us that Ursula was a widow with two grown children, Richard and Ania, so first cousins to me.

Armed with this information, Georgina immediately undertook some sleuthing and discovered that Richard and Ania were both on Facebook. With my agreement, she sent Richard the following message:

Dear Richard,

Please forgive the unsolicited message and my trespassing on your Facebook. I have been helping my adopted cousin search for her family for many years and you may be able to help us. My name is Georgina Milligan and my cousin is Krystyna

Bracey. Please feel free to check our Facebook profiles.

I am mindful of the sensitivities involved in engaging in such communication, but I wonder if the family name, Szafranska means anything to you. We are looking for siblings of a Krystyna Szafranska, who was born in 1929. We believe she had four other sisters, two who stayed in Poland and two others who came with her to England with their father, Maxymilian. We think the two with Krystyna were Ursula and Marylka.

It is a long shot but I found an Ursula Szafranska married Boleslaw Wasilkowski in the 50s and that in turn led me to you.

Do any of these names mean anything to you? I do apologise profusely if I have caused any offence or shock but we have been searching for over 20 years and only recently have had a small breakthrough. My cousin would love to find blood relatives. My email is... If this means nothing to you I again apologise for bothering you. Signed, Georgie Milligan.

Richard, a keen yachtsman, was sailing in the Mediterranean with his best friend, Edward, at this time. They just happened to be at anchor in the tranquil bay of Porto Palma, northern Sardinia, when Richard received Georgina's text via his Messenger. Having shared the text with Edward, who immediately thought the message was a scam, Richard decided to reply, asking for a contact telephone number. Georgina duly provided her number, and a short while later, she found herself talking to Richard.

Georgina explained the search she and I had been on and asked Richard a whole host of questions, to which she received an equal number of answers. Eventually, this led to Richard realising that he had a long-lost cousin who had been abandoned at birth by his favourite aunt and godmother, Krystyna.

As this revelation came to light, I was obliviously sitting in a cinema, which was not unusual for me since I love going to the pictures. When I came out, I rang Jeff as usual to let him know I was on my way home. He said that Georgina had rung and that I should ring her as soon as I could as she had some news for me.

Slightly apprehensive, I rang her and she excitedly told me that we had found my birth family. I was staggered and just couldn't believe it. After all this time, here she was telling me that she had had a long telephone conversation with Richard, my first cousin. She then quickly added that he had told her my birth mother, Krystyna - or Krysia as she had affectionately been known - had sadly passed away in Chicago in 1973. However, I still had two living aunts, one being Ursula or Ulka, as she was known, Richard's mother, and one in Kansas, Maria (also known as Marylka).

Even though I felt hugely excited at discovering my birth family, it was tinged with much sadness at the knowledge that I would never meet my birth mother.

Once home, Jeff met me at the door and gave me a huge hug. He was pleased for me but also concerned that I should not get too stressed at all the news I was receiving. The house phone rang almost immediately after this. I answered, and it was my newly discovered cousin, Richard. 'Hello cousin," he said, at which I became very emotional, as did Richard.

Our telephone conversation, needless to say, was a long one. It was interspersed with moments of tearfulness and laughter. Richard told me how special my mother, his aunt, had been to him. He said she had always been very generous to him and his sister, and that she loved to have fun and play tricks on them, creating much laughter and enjoyment. She was always so full of life. He recalled many visits to Hamleys toy shop, Harrods, and Fortnum and Mason, all in the company of his Ciocia (aunt) Krysia. In essence, he said, being Krysia's godson meant that he was quite spoilt. He went on to say that he was puzzled at how Krysia could have given me up, worse still, abandoned me because she had always displayed such a love of children.

Of course, no one would ever be able to give me a reason for being abandoned, as no body until now had known of my existence!

When Richard told me that he was Krysia's godson, I told him that, when I was a young girl I had an imaginary brother who I had named Richard. What a strange coincidence this turned out to be! Now I could call Richard my cousin, but also my god brother. He was very touched by this and said that he, in turn, would call me his new 'sis'.

Richard then said that he had rung his mother, Ursula, about me. When he told her about the discovery, she accused him of meddling on the 'worldwide web', which he vigorously denied. She then went on to say she could not believe that Krysia would not have told her of my existence. Richard responded by telling her that there was indisputable proof that I was indeed Krysia's daughter. Apparently, even though Ursula could not believe what Richard had told her, she rang her sister, Maria (Marylka), in Abilene, Kansas, to tell her the news.

Later that same evening, I received a phone call from Maria, or Ciocia Maria, as she introduced herself to me. She was tearful and very emotional and kept saying, "We never knew, we never knew." She could not understand how Krysia, even on her death bed, had never revealed to her that she had a daughter. She then went on to say that I should visit her in America, something I could never really envisage being able to do, but I knew that I would love to meet her if possible.

After I put the phone down, I rang Liam to tell him all the news. He was gobsmacked at all that had come to light. I told him I had agreed to meet Richard and I would very much like him to accompany me. He said he would be only too happy to come with me. He was blown away by everything I told him and was just as intrigued as I was to discover more.

I don't know how I went to bed that night. I spoke briefly to Georgina, thanking her for all that she had done so far in helping me. We even discussed the possibility of her meeting Richard with Liam and me. However, Georgina declined, saying that this was a time I needed to have to myself, as it was personal to me. She did, however, say that I should gather as much information as possible so that we could continue researching the family tree. She was so happy for me and was looking forward to learning a lot more about the Szafranska family.

Jeff and I talked long into the night. My head was buzzing with so many questions and an incredible sense of excitement.

As I lay my head on my pillow, my last thoughts were of Barbara. What would she have said?

Chapter 14

World War II - The Szafranska Story

Whilst I was fully aware of the devastating impact that World War II had brought about in this country, I was ignorant of the horrors that had befallen my birth family's country, Poland.

It began with Maxymilian Szafranski, born in 1895, who I now knew to be my maternal grandfather. Maxymilian lived in Inowraclaw, Poland, with his wife, Zofia, who was born in 1899. They had five daughters, Zosia, Genia, Krystyna (Krysia), Ursula, and Marylka (Maria).

Maxymilian was an officer in the Polish Army and had fought for the liberation of Poland in 1922. Seventeen years later, he found himself fighting again, this time as a consequence of the Second World War. Despite being captured by the invading Russian army, he miraculously escaped and joined the Polish Free Army (known as Anders' Army) under General Wladyslaw Anders.

As a result of the aggression between Germany and Russia, Poland faced genocide from both sides. The Polish military unsuccessfully fought against both the Nazis and the Russians. The German army was too strong for the Polish military, as they lacked troop numbers and equipment. As a result, Poland became a staging post for concentration camps. However, the Polish people continued to desire freedom despite facing unimaginable cruelty from their aggressors. Stalin accused the Polish people of attempting to undermine the Russian ideology and authority and issued orders for arrests and deportation of those Polish citizens he viewed as a threat.

The threat of deportation finally reached Zofia's front door early one cold morning in February 1940. Russian soldiers woke the family, banging the door with the butts of their rifles. When Zofia opened it, the soldiers shouted to her to gather her belongings and those of her children and that they were to leave their home within the hour. Marylka has told me that she and her sisters stood crying and screaming.

They were bewildered and frightened by the sight of the soldiers standing at the door in a menacing fashion. Zofia made her three daughters, Krystyna, aged 10, Ursula, aged 8, and Marylka, aged 5, dress in as many clothes as they could wear. She hurriedly gathered what food she could and also grabbed a goose down comforter (similar to a duvet). Zofia's two older daughters, Genia and Zosia, were living away from the house at this time. Genia was already married, and Zosia was working away as a school teacher. Somehow they managed to remain in Poland, but it was a different story for Zofia and her girls.

Zofia and her three daughters were made to march for a long time during the early hours of a dark morning until they finally reached a railway station. Here, they were greeted by many other Polish citizens, who were all in the same frightening and confusing situation. In front of them stood a long succession of cattle trucks headed by a large, steaming train. They were eventually herded onto these trucks, seventy to eighty people in each. There was no room to sit, only to stand. Zofia kept her three girls as close to her as possible, as people were jostled and pushed. In an unbelievable change of existence, they were now bound for the inhospitable region of Eastern Russia, Siberia. The train stood on the tracks for almost three days, during which time there was no food or water supplied. Overhead, planes could be heard dropping bombs, and this delayed their train in getting underway. Marylka still recalls how she tried to look through the gaps in the wooden slats of the truck. All she could see were throngs of people, mainly women and children. It was a frightening sight. Because of the close proximity of everyone, it was difficult to perform bodily functions. There were no toilet facilities, just a hole that had been cut in the corner of the truck. The stench of cramped humanity was almost too much to bear, but bear it they had to.

Once the train started to move, it was even worse, as the inhabitants of the cattle trucks found it hard to keep their footing as the truck swayed and rumbled over the tracks. Sleep was all but impossible. Despite their hunger, which was now intense, Zofia shared what meagre food she had with her children and also with others, foregoing food herself. It was the same for everyone; each tried to support the other.

Occasionally, the train would come to a halt, and an unbelievable sight met Marylka's curious young eyes as she once again looked through the slats of the truck. Bodies, including those of children and babies, who had perished on the journey, were slung unceremoniously out of the trucks into the snow-covered sidings. Marylka was speechless and shook with fear, afraid to tell anyone what she had seen.

Eventually, the family's gruelling ordeal of the journey was over, but a new one was to begin.

Marylka recalls getting off the train and standing with her mother and sisters, shivering with the intense cold. Once again, they were made to march. Where to, they did not know. Struggling through the deep snows of the Siberian wilderness was sheer torture. Their limbs felt numb, and the feeling of hunger was desperate and unbearable. Whenever they came to a halt in marching, they were allowed a watery soup, which served more as a drink than any form of nourishment. Finally, they reached the place that Zofia and her children had been assigned to live. If it could be called living! The house was a small hut-like building that housed a huge stove in one corner. The sole resident was an old Russian lady who lived in an impoverished state. She had been ordered to take in Polish citizens for re-education purposes. The house was extremely small; there was barely room for the family of four to sleep, so they slept top-to-tail under the goose-down comforter as best they could. The old lady occupied a bed in the opposite corner. She was not overly welcoming and did not offer any form of hospitality. In fact, she was equally in fear of the soldiers as they barked their orders at her. She only spoke Russian and wasn't very communicative, which made things very difficult and awkward for Zofia and the children. Zofia, along with many other Polish women and the older children, was put to work. She was sent out each day to strip bark from the many trees in the surrounding forest. It was a hard cruel task, made all the worse by the bitter cold. Food was extremely scarce. The old lady they lived with was not responsible for feeding the family that had been forced upon her. So, as Zofia was out working all day, it meant that Krysia, being the eldest sibling, would have to fetch the daily ration of food for them all. She had to endure standing for hours in long queues, just for a small amount of black bread and water. On the odd occasion, she would be fortunate enough to receive a solitary potato as well as the ration of bread. This was in no way sufficient to sustain the family, and Zofia would often go into the woods and dig up roots to boil and serve as soup. Ursula once told Richard that she had never endured such pain as that of sheer hunger. She said it was an unbearable pain, the like of which she had never known. As there was very little water for drinking or even washing, Zofia would often take icicles that hung from the roof and melt them down into drinking water. Almost two years of this harsh existence finally came to an end when, as a result of the Soviet Union joining the Allies after the Germans invaded Poland, an agreement was reached that brought freedom for the family and many others like them.

Once again, as the Polish people were allowed to leave the inhospitable plains of Siberia, Zofia and the girls found themselves marching through the bitterly cold winds and deep snows. The difference this time was that they were walking away from the horrific existence that they and others had endured for many months. Fortunately, they were eventually lucky enough to gain transport with a convoy of trucks. These trucks took them over very narrow, uneven roads on their way to the ships that would take them to Iran (or Persia as it was known at that time). Marylka remembers how scary the journey was as the trucks made their way across the mountainous track towards the sea. There was only room for one-way traffic. If a vehicle appeared ahead, they would have to reverse back along the treacherous road. Eventually, they reached the Caspian Sea. They were a raggle-taggle group of people amongst many others, all in the same situation. The Red Cross began ordering these unfortunate and weary people into formal lines in order to embark on the numerous large ships that were waiting on the edge of the waters. Zofia and her daughters were, by this time, exhausted, dirty and extremely hungry. Near starvation had left them barely able to walk or even to talk, but help was now at hand as they were led onto a ship to start their sea journey. The sea brought its own troubles by way of terrible seasickness. The turbulence of the waters and the swaying of the ship were almost as bad as what they had endured in Siberia.

At last, they reached the Persian shoreline of Pahlavi. As they disembarked, they were taken to a makeshift city consisting of many tents, which had been provided by the Iranian army. Zofia and her family were like so many others who had joined the great exodus to this land. They were all unrecognisable as the women and children they had once been. Instead, they resembled walking skeletons, their clothing mostly reduced to rags, and their bodies riddled with lice. Like so many others, Marylka and Ursula were showered, deloused, and had their heads shaved in the interest of hygiene. Miraculously, Krysia did not endure losing her hair. She showered and was given fresh clothes, as was Zofia.

After such a long time without proper nourishment, when the girls were presented with food, they could not contain their hunger, and they stuffed themselves so much that they became violently sick. Their distended stomachs could not cope with food, so they had to be slowly introduced to eating properly again. Some of their fellow refugees died purely from overeating.

Sadly, although the family found themselves away from the horrors of the war and ill treatment they had received, Zofia contracted tuberculosis, no doubt as a result of the harsh conditions she had endured and her sacrificing her own food to give to her children. This inevitably took a toll on her body. She died in August 1942, aged 43, and her grave is marked in the Polish Military Cemetery in Tehran, which to this day is tended by the Polish Government. This tragic loss of their mother meant the girls were now effectively orphans.

The Red Cross managed to make contact with their father, Maxymilian, who was, by this time, fighting in Africa. They informed him of the death of his wife, and having been given compassionate leave, Maxymilian was able to join his daughters for the funeral.

Krysia, Ursula and Marylka were now motherless. Their father requested the Red Cross to make arrangements for his daughters to be sent to an orphanage in Tanganyika under the care of the Sisters of Nazareth, a Catholic missionary serving several parts of Africa.

When the girls were ready to be transported on another ship to Africa, Marylka began to show signs of a fever and was removed from the ship. Krysia and Ursula were, for a time, unaware that this had happened, but as the ship was underway, there was nothing they could do other than alert the relevant authorities that their sister was missing. Marylka was later to find herself, by some means or another, in New Zealand! She has told me since that her mind is a blank as to what happened thereafter. It is possible that she was suffering from a form of shock. When Maxymilian was made aware of what had happened, he requested that the Red Cross help to reunite Marylka with her two sisters, and eventually, they were all together again. They were then moved to an orphanage, which was based at the Rongai Camp in Kenya.

From the harsh surroundings they had inhabited in Siberia, the girls now found themselves basking under the beautiful, warm sunlit skies of Kenya.

At the camp, as Krysia being the elder of her two siblings, was educated with peers of her own age group. Ursula and Marylka were taught with the other younger orphans. A uniform was provided to wear for school. Marylka remembers clearly that during the week they would wear grey and white blouses over their skirts, and on Sundays they would wear blue and white blouses. Lessons were basic, and they were mainly taught in Polish but also learnt English as a second language. Marylka has admitted that she was not a good scholar, preferring to disappear and explore the incredible landscape that surrounded the camp.

The sisters, along with many other children, were fascinated by the sight of the abundant wildlife that roamed in the midst of their surroundings. They gazed in wonderment at such wonderful creatures as elephants, giraffes, gazelles, and even lions. Of course, safety at the camp was paramount, but it did not stop the curious youngsters exploring further into the countryside than they should! Fascinating termite hills, tall enough to climb, were dotted about and provided a popular pastime when playing. The food that was provided was much more nourishing, and as the months passed, the children began to regain their strength. The constant sunshine was an added tonic for them.

The three sisters spent the duration of the war and beyond in this fascinating environment and enjoyed much laughter and fun, something they had missed since leaving their homeland. When the war came to an end in 1945, they remained in Kenya until the powers-that-be started to organise repatriation for everyone.

Towards the end of 1947, Maxymilian asked Krysia, as the eldest of the girls, to decide where the family should settle since it would not be possible for them to remain in Kenya.

He asked her whether she would like to return to Poland or take the opportunity of going to Australia, the USA, or England. Krysia chose England. So it was that in February 1948, she and her two sisters travelled to Mombasa, where they boarded the SS Caernarvon Castle, which in May 1948 finally docked at Banana Wharf in Southampton. From here, they were transferred to a refugee camp in Yorkshire. A few months later, along with their father, Maxymilian, the family of four moved to another camp. They moved to a camp at Fairford, near Cirencester, where at last their new life in the country they would now call home could begin.

The family would never forget what they had endured, and they certainly would never forget their mother, but a new life, in a new country, now beckoned.

Chapter 15

A long-awaited meeting

Following the joy at finding my birth family, I was in awe to hear what they had endured during the war. I could not believe what my birth mother, Krysia, had had to cope with during her childhood and teenage years. Barbara had often told me tales of her war-time experiences in the ATS, but they paled into insignificance with what Krysia and her family had gone through. I couldn't wait to finally meet my Aunt Ursula, and hear first-hand about the family, and in particular about Krysia's life.

In early June 2017, I journeyed to London and stayed with Liam and Jane. I was very excited at the prospect of finally meeting members of my birth family, but at the same time, I was filled with nervous tension. I had to fight the butterflies that started to invade my tummy.

Liam and I set off to see Richard and his mother, Ursula. Richard's home was in Esher, where we had agreed to meet. As as we approached Richard's house, which was set on a long road that overlooked the racecourse, Sandown Park, we both sensed a degree of apprehension. Liam looked at me and gave me a reassuring smile saying, "You'll be alright, mum; I'm with you on this." He, like me, was still reeling from the fact that after so many years of very little knowledge of my birth background, suddenly everything had snowballed. Now here we were on the verge of meeting blood family.

Upon arriving at Richard's house, there was no one at home. I rang him, worried that I might be at the wrong place. When Richard answered, he apologised for not being there to greet us and said that he had had to pick up his mother. He said he would be with us in a short while. Sure enough, within minutes a car arrived on the driveway. Richard got out and immediately hugged me and then shook hands with Liam. He had a welcoming smile on his well-tanned, pleasant features. He wore glasses and had greying, cropped hair. From the side of the car, Richard's mother appeared. A tiny, fragile-looking lady stood in front of me. She had slightly wavy, light-coloured hair, worn with a side parting held back by a slide. She was wearing large-framed glasses and was standing with her arms folded across her chest, a carrier bag swinging from her arm. She looked at me and, in a defensive manner, uttered the words, "'I don't know anything." With this remark, she scurried through Richard's front door.

Richard, sensing the awkwardness between us, ushered Liam and me into his house. Ursula made a bee-line for the kitchen. As Richard invited us to take a seat on his comfy looking brown leather sofa, I surveyed the long length of his sitting room. An impressive looking marble fireplace stood opposite us. The room was very inviting, with terracotta painted walls. At the back of us, hanging on a pole, was a beautiful kilim, a Persian-style rug in blue and orange hues, which picked up the colour of the surrounding walls. My eyes were suddenly drawn to a bookcase opposite, on which stood a bronze-coloured Grecian-style urn. It was adorned with candles, beside which stood a framed photograph that I recognised as being of my birth mother, Krysia.

Richard had followed my eyes. He told me that the urn contained Krysia's ashes. "Really," I said as I got up and walked across the room, a lump rising in my throat. I reached up and touched the urn, saying quietly to myself, "Hello Mum." I realised I was shaking with a heartfelt sadness. It was unbelievable that after all the years of never knowing who my mother was, I was now touching the last vestige of her. I felt deeply privileged that I had been blessed with the opportunity of reaching out to her, albeit only by virtue of her ashes. As I said a silent prayer, I noticed that the name engraved on the urn read Krystyna T. Menkin. I turned to Richard and asked what the initial T stood for. He answered that it stood for Teresa. I was speechless, as this was the same middle name that Barbara and Bill had given me when I was adopted. Theresa had been Bill's mother's name. Two names now strongly resonated with me; first Richard, my make-believe brother, and now Teresa, although a different spelling. What an amazing coincidence.

Ursula came in from the kitchen and hesitantly sat down beside me. She was as nervous as me about all that had evolved. I realised that, by coming into her life, she had been left asking herself a lot of questions about her sister, Krysia. As sisters, she had thought that she and Krysia knew each other well. Now here I was, proof that this was not the case. I started to tell Richard and Ursula about my life, how I had been brought up by Barbara and Bill, my adoptive parents. To aid my story,

I showed them several photos of me as a young child and teenager. I also produced my original birth certificate, which showed how Krysia had registered my birth in early January 1953 and how she had given the false surname of Franska. Ursula said, "I don't understand; Krysia loved children. How could she have had a baby without us knowing?" I then produced my adoption papers showing that Krysia had left me just two and half weeks after giving birth to me. By this time, I could sense that my voice was beginning to get shaky, as I was so nervous. I said that I had long desired to discover my birth family. At this, Ursula suddenly caught hold of my hand, squeezing it tightly and saying, "It's alright, my darling. It's all been such a shock to us; we honestly never knew." Suddenly, I began to relax, and I felt that I was now truly being accepted as Krysia's secret daughter.

Richard produced a bottle of Veuve Clicquot, a favourite champagne of his and Ursula's, to celebrate our finding one another. Along with this, Richard served us a selection of savoury foods: salami, sun-dried tomatoes, artichokes, and olives. Sadly, I was not a fan of this sort of fare. Not wishing to embarrass Richard, I picked at a few pieces, hoping he would not notice. Richard went on to open a bottle of wine, Sauvignon Blanc, which Ursula and I, unbeknownst to me, managed to finish by the end of the evening. Liam was driving, so he only partook of a soft drink, and Richard too abstained. Having eaten and drunk, Richard got out his laptop and began to share some footage of an old cine film with us all. Suddenly, I found myself looking at moving images in black and white. They were images of my birth mother and Leslie, Krysia's husband. I couldn't believe it, especially when Liam said, "Mum, she is so like you." He was right. It was like looking at myself, the mannerisms, the way she stood, even her smile was so like mine. The only thing I was sorry about was that the film was silent. It would have been marvellous to have heard Krysia's voice. But I was still moved beyond words by what I had seen.

Suddenly I felt a sadness because I would never actually know my birth mother, but I was elated by the fact of how alike we seemed to be. This made me determined to learn as much as possible about her from Ursula and Marylka.

Ursula told me a little about Krysia, as she affectionately called her. She briefly touched on their experience as children growing up in the Second World War but said she would tell me more on another occasion. She added that when Krysia had grown up, she had yearned for the good life and eventually found this by going to live in London. She told me that, one day, she would show me where Krysia and her husband had lived. She then invited Liam and me to her house for tea the following day.

Richard took several photographs of us all, saying it would serve as a record of our meeting. A little later, it was time to say goodbye after what had turned out to be an awesome evening. As we would be passing Ursula's house on the way back, Liam offered to give her a lift home, which she happily accepted.

As we set off after what had been a full evening, I began to feel a little unwell. I suspect that the consumption of alcohol and little food had caught up with me! As we pulled up at Ursula's house, I suddenly flung open my car door and proceeded to be very unwell. I was so embarrassed. Ursula stood watching me in disbelief. She was very sympathetic and kept saying, "You poor dear, you poor dear." Eventually, as I began to feel a little better, Liam and I said a final goodbye. He was very watchful of me as we continued our journey home. Once there, I can honestly say that I do not remember much about going to bed. The following morning, I couldn't believe it when I found myself on my bed, still fully dressed. I really had let myself down.

My mobile phone suddenly rang; it was Ursula asking how I was feeling. She said she was so sorry and that she had been worried at seeing me in such a state. I assured her that I was fine now and that it had probably been due to a combination of excitement and lack of food. We both agreed that we were looking forward to meeting again later that day.

Poor Liam, what an embarrassment I must have been to him, but he made nothing of it when I saw him later that morning. He was just relieved that I appeared to be my normal self again.

Later that day, Liam and I set off to Ursula's house, taking with us a lovely bunch of flowers for her. When we arrived, she greeted us with warm enthusiasm and was delighted with the floral bouquet. "Come in, come in," she said and led us through her house and into the garden. It was a lovely, sunny day, and Ursula took great pleasure in showing us her many rose bushes, all of which were heavily festooned with flowers. As we went back into the house, Richard appeared. He said he wouldn't be staying but just wanted to say hello again and wish me a good journey home the following day. He said that he would look forward very much to seeing me again before long. A short while later, Ursula took us into her front room, in the middle of which was a large oval table, covered in a white tablecloth and laid out for a meal. As we sat down, the front door opened, and a voice called out. It was Ania, Richard's sister, with her daughter, Rebecca. Rebecca greeted Ursula, saying, "Hello, Babcha." This was the phrase for a grandmother in Polish. I was touched by this as it seemed such an affectionate word. Ania greeted Liam and me, saying how lovely it was to finally meet. She was a tall and attractive lady with bright auburn hair and a bubbly personality to go with it. Rebecca was also good-looking, very slim, with long, blonde hair. I found myself fascinated by her wonderful eyelashes; she was definitely a fan of make-up!

Ursula served us homemade Polish chicken soup, which was so delicious that both Liam and I had a second helping. This was followed by another popular Polish food, pierogi, which Ursula had prepared. They were little dumplings filled with either cheese or spinach and meat. During the course of the meal, Ania suddenly passed a photograph to me. I took one look and was totally unprepared by my reaction, which was to burst into tears. I was looking at a beautiful photograph of Krysia with her husband, Leslie. They had been captured as they were dancing at a party, and Krysia looked so beautiful with a gorgeous smile on her face and her husband looking down at her adoringly. I couldn't believe how Krysia's face bore a strong resemblance to me in my early twenties. Liam was taken aback by my sudden emotional state and tried to comfort me. Then Ursula surprised me too; she had been searching in a cupboard of a tall display cabinet. Suddenly she produced a pencil portrait of Krysia, which was signed Roy 58. Just who Roy was, I still have not discovered. The portrait was beautiful, and once again, it bore a strong resemblance between Krysia and me. The portrait now sits in pride of place in my sitting room.

There could certainly be no doubt now as to who my birth mother was. I think, at that moment, everyone realised that Krysia had long harboured a huge secret and that this secret had gone to her grave.

The evening ended all too fast and we had to take our leave, saying farewell but not goodbye.

Liam was fascinated by everything that we had discovered and by the knowledge that he now had blood-related cousins. Of course, the cousins we had through my adoptive family would always remain number one for us. We would never ever lose the strong bond we shared.

The weekend had turned out to be a remarkable, celebratory occasion. It was the culmination of many years of searching and yearning to know who I really was. Now, I felt a completeness in my life that I had never had.

There was still be more to learn about Krysia, and I was looking forward to hearing about her from Ursula. We had both agreed that I would arrange to visit and stay with my new Ciocia Ursula very soon.

Chapter 16

Footsteps in the past

Following my unbelievable meeting with Ciocia (Aunt) Ursula and cousins Richard and Ania in June 2017, I began to enjoy further contact with them by telephone, FaceTime, and occasional letters.

Cousin Roger in America was delighted to learn that I had been fortunate to make successful contact with members of his grandmother's long-lost family. He told me that he and Kathy would be undertaking a cruise around Europe in August and wondered whether I would be able to meet them in Liverpool, where they were due to dock. Although they would only be there for a day, it meant that we would have the opportunity to actually meet in person. Excitedly, I made arrangements with Georgina to stay overnight with her in Yorkshire so that we could travel together to Liverpool the following day. After all the support and help Georgina had given me in my search for my birth family, I wanted her to meet Roger. After all, had it not been for him contacting me, I could still have been searching. Unfortunately, illness prevented me from travelling, so it was with great sadness that I had to put our much-anticipated meeting off. I had suffered another TIA, which meant I did not feel safe to travel for a few weeks. I was deeply disappointed at the knowledge that now I would never have an opportunity of meeting Roger. My illness was also to prevent me from taking my promised trip to Ursula, planned for early October.

It was not until May of the following year that I was finally able to travel and stay with Ciocia Ursula. I spent my coach journey wondering how much I would be able to glean from her about my birth mother, Krystyna, or Krysia as she was fondly referred to by the family. The weekend happened to coincide with the wedding of Prince Harry and Meghan Markle. I did not, however, anticipate that we would be joining the crowds at Windsor for the occasion. My main desire was to explore the areas of London that had a particular resonance with Krysia and her past life.

On arrival at Victoria Coach Station, I found Ursula waiting for me. I sensed an initial nervousness between us as we greeted one other, but soon Ursula gave me a warm smile which put me at ease. She linked arms with me as we made our way to her home in Ealing. Once there, Ursula immediately showed me upstairs to my bedroom so that I could settle in. She said that the bedroom was where Krysia used to stay whenever she visited. I viewed the dark brown furniture, so familiar in homes of the 50s and 60s, which I remembered from my childhood. It was a large, comfortable room, with floral patterned paper adorning the walls. There were several pretty pictures of flowers and attractive scenes of Polish life long ago. I was struck by the very high single bed, which was situated sideways against one of the walls. I smiled to myself as I envisaged how I would later manage to climb into it! On the dressing table, I found that Ursula had left me some sweets on a pretty dish decorated with giraffes.

The sweets were Polish chocolates with fruit centres. I was touched that Ursula had remembered that I had a sweet tooth. She had previously told me that Krysia, too, had been a lover of sweets.

After I had relaxed for an hour or so, Ursula took me into the centre of London, where we headed towards Trafalgar Square. It was a lovely way to spend the sunny evening, and there were plenty of people who, like us, were taking in the sights and sounds of the city. We proceeded to walk through China Town, which was a place I had never been to before, despite having lived in London when I was first married. I thoroughly enjoyed the evening, and as the sun began to set, we returned to Ursula's home, where we relaxed and chatted over a glass of wine before retiring to bed.

As eager as I was to find out as much as possible about Krysia, I felt that it was not quite the right time to bombard Ursula with the many questions I had. Instead, I told her I was looking forward to her taking me to see some of the places that had been familiar to Krysia when she had lived in London. Ursula told me that Krysia had loved her life in London and that she would show me where Krysia and Leslie had actually lived. With the mention of Leslie's name, I couldn't help but ask the question that had been at the back of my mind ever since discovering that he had married Krysia. I asked whether or not Leslie Corke could be my father. She quickly dismissed this idea with a wave of her hand, saying, "No, no." It was immediately evident that Ursula was not prepared to be drawn into a conversation on the subject as she abruptly bid me good night. I hoped that I had not upset her, but I was determined to try and find answers about my birth.

The following morning, after a good night's sleep, I awoke to see sunlight streaming through my window. As I started to move, I was aware of the sound of classical music playing loudly downstairs. After dressing, I made my way down to the kitchen where I found Ursula, or Ulka as she was often called, drinking a cup of tea. I greeted her, saying that I too enjoyed listening to classical music. She said that she always had her radio tuned to Classic FM whenever she was at home. She added that she loved going to live classical concerts, particularly those at the Royal Albert Hall. After breakfast, we made our way to the underground station, which was just a short walk from Ursula's house. It was another lovely sunny day with a cloudless blue sky. We travelled to Earls Court, where we disembarked. Ursula was a fast walker, and I found myself hurrying to keep up with her as I had the night before. Eventually, after wending our way through a maze of streets, she took me into a small roadway just off Cromwell Road. The road sign read Kenway Road, SW5. Suddenly, Ursula stopped in front of a building and said, "This is where Krysia and Leslie lived, in the flat up there," as she pointed in an upward direction. I found myself looking at a plain-looking front door painted red, through which one could make entry to the flat. A strange feeling came over me as I realised I was treading where once my mother had trod. Kenway Road was a quiet, attractive, mews-like area. It struck me as a peaceful and pleasant place. Ursula told me that the flat had been quite large and that there was also a courtyard at the back where Richard and Ania used to play as children when visiting their favourite aunt. I could not believe that I was standing exactly where my life may possibly have started. My mind flitted to Barbara and Bill when they lived in the same area of London as Krysia in the early 1950s. Did they ever meet my mother? Could they ever have met one another in the Rose & Crown pub in Hammersmith when Barbara and Bill ran it? Questions I knew I would never have answers to, but it set my mind reeling with wild imagination. Ursula pulled me back from my reverie as she took me by the arm and led me away from Kenway Road. I looked back and took a photograph to remind me of where I had been; it was all so amazing. I had finally visited a place that had a connection to my birth mother, and I found it quite overwhelming.

Ursula began to walk quickly once again. This time we were heading towards the bustling area of Knightsbridge. On the way, we passed The Church of the Immaculate Heart of Mary, otherwise known as the Brompton Oratory, one of the most prestigious Catholic churches in London. This was the place where Ursula and Boleslaw had been married in 1958. It was also where Richard had been christened, on which occasion Krysia had become his godmother. Tears began to moisten my eyes as I quickly turned to Ursula and asked if we could go inside. I wanted to pause here for a while in order to light a candle in memory of Krysia, my birth mother whom I never knew. Ursula was more than happy to go inside and led me through the vast, beautiful interior, which smelt strongly of incense and highly polished pews. It was a magnificent place, full of reverence and peacefulness that was suited to my emotions at that moment. I lit a candle and placed it in front of one of the beautiful altars that surrounded the walls. As I did so, I was transported back to my childhood. I thought of the many times I had prayed in my local church about who my birth parents might be and whether they would ever come looking for me. After a period of contemplation, we took our leave. As I walked down the steps of the church, I felt as though I was in a trance. Everything I had experienced so far seemed so surreal.

There were many thoughts running through my mind as Ursula walked me towards a nearby bus stop; from here, we caught a bus that would take us to Brompton Road. When we arrived, Ursula walked me to Harrods and asked if I wanted to go in. She said it had always been one of Krysia's favourite stores. Although I had been here several times myself, as well as with Barbara and Liam, it felt different this time. As we walked about in the store, I sensed how it must have felt to Krysia, and it made me realise how she must have enjoyed the prestige of shopping in this wonderful place.

London was buzzing with excitement; shops were festooned with decorations and memorabilia for the wedding of Prince Harry and Meghan Markle. People all around were talking about the celebrations. Had I been at home, I would no doubt have watched the ceremony on television. I found Ursula looking at me, and as if reading my mind, she said, "We can watch the highlights on television later."

By the time we had walked what felt like the length and breadth of London, we finally headed home. Thankfully, Ursula suggested we take a bus. What music that was to my ears, as I had begun to feel quite weary. I could not believe Ursula's stamina at the age of 86; she was amazing.

When we reached home, Ursula could see how tired I was, especially as I had nearly fallen asleep on the bus! She told me to go upstairs and have a rest whilst she prepared the evening meal. I needed no encouragement and headed up to my bedroom to lie down. Despite revelling in the day's experiences, sleep quickly stole over me. An hour or so later, I awoke and, as I lay looking up at the ceiling, I could hardly believe that I had been given such an insight into Krysia's life. I thought back to my time in 1973, when I had lived in Shepherds Bush and Chelsea during my first marriage. If I had only known then that I had blood family living in such close proximity, perhaps life would have turned out differently for me. But fate did not play her hand at that time.

When I went downstairs, I found Ursula busy preparing Zander, a fish I had never heard of. Ursula told me it was a popular perch-like fish much enjoyed in Poland. When we ate later, I found it to be a delicate, white fish, and Ursula had cooked it to perfection as it melted in my mouth. I tentatively broached the subject of her experience during the war years. Unfortunately, she seemed reluctant to talk about this. She did, however, suddenly disappear into the living room and returned holding a large book. The book had a black, glossy cover and was entitled Exiled Children.

Ursula turned the pages quickly, telling me that it was an account of how the Polish orphans were cared for by the nuns in the Catholic-run orphanages in Kenya during the war. Incredibly, I was suddenly looking at a photo of two young girls; it was Ursula and her sister, Maria. As I continued to look at the many photos, they left me in awe of what Krysia and her sisters must have experienced. I thought of how hard it must have been for Krysia when, at the age of 13, she had had to comfort her two younger sisters when their mother tragically passed away. With all that she had already gone through in Siberia and beyond, she must have suddenly felt abandoned and frightened. How could she have explained her feelings to her two younger siblings? It was certainly an unenviable situation to be in. I decided that, once I returned home, I would look at my adoption papers again. With what I had found out from my visit, I wanted to see if I could get a better idea as to what had led to me being abandoned.

My stay with Ursula came to an end all too quickly, and it was with a certain reluctance that I journeyed home. I felt that I had not asked all the questions I needed answers to, but I also realised that there was a certain reluctance on Ursula's part to talk about Krysia. Was it because she was afraid of letting the cat out of the bag? I would need to take things gently with her on the delicate issue surrounding my birth. When I arrived home, I regaled Jeff with all that I had found out and seen. Jeff could sense that I was totally animated by everything I had experienced. He laughingly said, "You should write a book about this. It is an incredible tale." He added that he was convinced that Barbara may well have known more than she ever told me about the circumstances of my adoption.

I looked forward to paying Ursula another visit before long when I would hopefully learn more. For now, I felt privileged to have gained a degree of knowledge about Krysia's life, which I had been unaware of just a few years ago.

Sadly, just six weeks later, on 30th June, I was stunned to receive a phone call from Richard to tell me that Ursula had suddenly passed away. She had been staying at Milford-on-Sea with a long-time friend. She had gone to bed and never woke up. Whilst it turned out to be a peaceful passing, it was a massive shock to her friends and family, including me. I could not believe that I would no longer be able to talk to Ursula about Krysia. It was an extremely sad moment for me. I asked Richard if I could attend Ursula's funeral, to which he replied, "Of course, you are her niece." He then told me that Ursula's sister, Maria, would be flying over for the funeral, together with her two daughters, Susan and Darlene.

Suddenly, amidst all the sadness and disappointment that my quest to discover more about my newly-found family was over, another door had opened. I would be able to meet my other aunt, and maybe, just maybe, she would be able to tell me more about Krysia. It was a bittersweet moment as I realised that, by losing one aunt, I would now have the opportunity of meeting the other. My heart began to lift at the thought.

Chapter 17

Understanding Krysia

Following the shocking news of Ursula's unexpected death, Richard rang me to say that her funeral would be on 23rd July. I could not believe my ears when I heard the date; it was the same date as mum's birthday. I would never be able to forget that date, would I?

I journeyed once again to London and stayed with Liam and Jane in advance of the funeral. Liam had been astounded by the incredible story that had unravelled since first discovering my blood family. We chatted at length about everything that had occurred since mum's death. I still bore a sense of guilt about her because of searching for my birth family, but I also knew that my adoptive family were happy and supported me in my quest. Liam said that, by throwing myself into searching for my birth mother, he believed it had helped me with the loss of the person who had been my lifetime mum. As much as she had made me feel forever beholden to her in respect of my adoption, it felt like an epiphany to finally be free to discover where my roots lay. Perhaps it was serendipity!

The following day, Liam, Jane and I met Richard and the family at a pub near Ursula's home. By a strange coincidence, the pub was called The Rose and Crown, the same name as the pub my parents had run in Hammersmith in 1951. It was here that I came face-to-face with Krysia's youngest sister, Marylka (known as Maria), and her two daughters. As Richard led us through to the dining area, I started to feel nervous.

It was an emotional moment as Maria stood up to greet me and enfolded me in her arms. We both wept tears of pent-up emotion, not only because of the sad occasion that had brought us together but also because Maria was finally meeting her niece that she had never known existed. After hugging, she held me at arms length and said, "You have the Szafranska hips." If only mum could have been a fly on the wall. She had taunted me so often about my Polish appearance, referring to me unkindly as a Polish washerwoman. I still remain mystified as to why she used this expression and wish she had referred to my Polish heritage in a kinder manner.

Maria was taller than Ursula and was of a similar build to me. She wore her slightly greying hair in pretty short curls, which suited her good looks. I observed that she wore pretty drop earrings from her pierced ears and that she had several silver bracelets adorning her wrists. Her attractive nails were beautifully painted. I immediately felt that we were similar in our appearance. After greeting one another, I found myself in turn being hugged by Susan and Darlene, another two first cousins I had now finally met. It was certainly a large gathering of my newly-found family as Richard's daughter, Kamila, and her two children, Quinn and Oscar, had also joined us. I had already met Kamila when I stayed with Ursula. Little did I think that I would see her again so soon. If anyone had told me that I would finally be in the midst of my birth family at the age of 65, I would never have believed it. I was completely overwhelmed by the whole experience, even more so when Maria suddenly took one of her silver bracelets off her wrist and handed it to me. She said, "Now you have something of me to keep." I was deeply touched by her words and admired the lovely bracelet, which I immediately placed on my wrist. She then promised that once she was back home in Kansas, she would send me some pieces of Krysia's jewellery that she had kept. Again, I couldn't believe how things were evolving.

After much talking and enjoying a family meal, everyone eventually said their farewells. The next time we would all meet would be for a final goodbye to a much loved mother, sister and aunt.

The day before the funeral, Richard came to pick me up to stay with him overnight. This was so that I could travel to the funeral in company with him and Alex, his young son. Alex lived with his mother in Poland and was visiting his father for the summer holidays. Richard had brought him to Devon to meet Jeff and me in the summer of 2017, after Liam and I had gone to Esher in early June. When I arrived at Richard's home, I was greeted by Alex with an enthusiastic hug. Also staying there was a family friend, Mikolaj. He had travelled from Poland to attend the funeral on behalf of his family. He was extremely tall, well-built and good looking, with dark hair surrounding a square face. He spoke good English and immediately put me at ease. Richard told me that Mikolaj's mother was called Krystyna and that she and her late husband had been good friends with the Szafranska family when they lived in Poland before the war. Mikolaj 's father had been a vet, a career that he too had followed, and now had his own practice in Poland. Later, we all had an enjoyable evening meal, courtesy of Richard's culinary skills.

A bright, sunny day greeted us for the occasion of Ursula's funeral, which everyone was grateful for. I found this a comfort as I have always felt happier at seeing the sun on the day of a funeral, believing it to be a good sign for those departing this world.

The funeral service was held in Polish at the same Catholic Church that I had attended with Ursula only a few weeks ago. It was a strange experience for me, as I found myself sitting in a pew on my own. It was not intentional, but the immediate family just happened to be clustered together. I did not mind sitting alone as the Polish language was lost on me. I tried to follow the service as much as possible but found myself drifting in my thoughts. I could hardly believe that so much had happened in the past year or so. It all seemed somewhat surreal.

At the end of the service, I made my way outside. I felt a bit lost as members of the congregation surrounded the family, offering their condolences in their native tongue. Suddenly, an attractive lady came running towards me. She was short in stature, with greying blonde short-bobbed hair, which suited her round, smiling, smooth-skinned face. She stopped in front of me and placed a hand on my arm, saying, "I knew your mother and your father; we used to have such fun." I was staggered, here was someone telling me not only about my birth mother but also my father, or so I thought! As I stood staring at her, I said, "Yes, I am Krystyna's secret daughter." Suddenly, I had no other words; I was so taken aback by this lady's revelation. There was no time to talk any further as the funeral procession was preparing to move off to the crematorium. I looked about for Richard but was ushered into a minibus for the journey, which made me feel slightly ill at ease as, despite knowing that I was part of the family, I suddenly felt left out. I told myself I was being melodramatic and to shake myself out of it.

Following the committal of Ursula at the Mortlake Crematorium in Kew, the family and friends were invited for refreshments at the Lowiczanka Restaurant in the well-known Polish Centre in Hammersmith. Once there, excited at the thought that there was someone who could tell me more about my parentage, I scanned the many people who were milling around. I finally came across the lady who had greeted me with such exuberance. She was standing with her husband and greeted me warmly, saying her name was Lodzia. She briefly told me that she, too, had been in Africa during the war, and this was how she had become a lifetime friend with the Szafranska sisters. She told her husband to give me their telephone number so that I would be able to talk to her at a more appropriate time. Shortly after our brief conversation, they made their excuses to the family and took their leave to return to their home in Swindon.

My newly-found cousin, Susan, came over to me and steered me towards the table where other family members were sitting. We all chatted affably about things in general before heading back to Ursula's house.

My mind was buzzing with questions that I wanted to ask Maria about Krysia's life. Unfortunately, I did not manage to have any quiet time with her, and all too soon, I was heading back to Richard's house with Alex and Mikolaj. It had been an eventful day, but I found myself feeling disappointed by the lack of new information about Krysia.

The following day, as I journeyed back home by coach, my mind drifted to my birth mother and how things might have transpired in her short life.

I thought of how Krysia and her sisters had arrived in England in 1948. It must have been exciting but also bewildering for them. A voyage across the sea from the warmth of Africa to the chill of an English spring must have come as a bit of a shock. At that time, there would have been no relation to turn to, just the reliance of the British Red Cross, which helped many of the refugees who, like Krysia and her sisters, were all embarking on new lives in England. It must have been with much relief that the girls were finally joined by their father, Maxymilian. Together at last, the family began to rebuild their lives as they settled into a Polish Resettlement Camp. This was one of many that were run by the National Assistance Board throughout the UK after the war to help the many thousands of displaced Polish men, women and children searching for a new life. After spending a brief period of time in Yorkshire, the family moved to a camp near Fairford on the fringes of the Cotswolds. It was one of the largest camps in the country. Krysia by this time was nearly 20 and, as with most young people of that age, longed to be independent. She had always been artistic, and I learnt from Maria that Krysia had enrolled at the Swindon College School of Art and Design. It was whilst in Swindon that she began to feel the urge to spread her wings, which led her to London. I imagine that she must have heard about the city and longed for a taste of London life herself. How she eventually arrived in London, I have not been unable to discover, but arrive she did.

I have no idea how Krysia managed to find somewhere to live or where she may have worked. From some conversations with Maria, I learnt that she felt Krysia was a bit of a social butterfly. There is no denying that Krysia was an attractive young lady and must have turned many a suitor's head!

At some point during Krysia's time in London, she struck up a friendship with an American soldier whose name was Irvin Menkin. He was born in Iowa in the United States in 1914. His parents were Russian Jews who had emigrated to America in the early 1900s. Irvin was tall, with dark hair and brown eyes. Krysia was attracted to Irvin, even though he was fifteen years older than her. I understand from various research that Irvin had served in the Second World War, and at some point, he was in Japan. I have a photograph of Irvin, which was passed to me by Richard. It sits in an embossed leather frame which Krysia had bought from Harrods. I do not know what transpired between Irvin and Krysia or whether there was ever a romantic liaison. I later discovered that, at some point in their friendship, Irvin returned to America, where he lived for many years, but continued to keep in contact with Krysia.

Krysia thoroughly embraced her new lifestyle in London. She loved the big shops, the wonderful restaurants, and the theatres. Much to Krysia's delight, she loved the fact that London was a haven of fashion. She loved wearing the latest stylish clothes and even enjoyed designing and making her own on occasion. She also had a penchant for jewellery and antiques and became quite the expert on silver items.

Maria also told me that Krysia liked to paint in watercolours, something that I, too, have dabbled in. Her designer gene has, I think, passed to Liam, which I am delighted about.

Krysia happily enjoyed her whirlwind social life, and before long, she met and fell in love with Leslie Corke, a commercial designer who was five years her senior. There was just one problem, he was married, and furthermore, he had two young children. However, this did nothing to quell their desire for one another. Within a short time, Krysia and Leslie began living together. This was something that Krysia's father would never have condoned, given her Catholic faith. A chance visit by one of Krysia's sisters, Genia, who had travelled from Poland to visit her father and sisters, brought Maxymilian's attention to the fact that Krysia was, in effect, living in sin. Despite her father's anger and disappointment, Krysia refused to give Leslie up.

In early 1952, Krysia fell pregnant, the result of which was her giving birth to me at the end of December. Whatever the circumstances of my conception, I now take the view that, given the horrors Krysia had experienced in her very young life and the anger and disappointment that she would probably have caused her father, she found it impossible to reveal the truth to anyone in the family.

It is hard to contemplate just how Krysia dealt with the dilemma of being pregnant or how she managed to keep it a secret from her siblings. Ursula told me that she had a vague recollection that one particular Christmas, Krysia was not present at the traditional family gathering on Christmas Eve, which is a very important occasion in the Polish calendar. All family members gather for a big feast, followed by the giving and receiving of presents. Ursula told me that although Krysia did not attend, she gave no reason or excuse for her absence. This would almost certainly have been because by this time, she was all but ready to give birth. Krysia gave birth to me on 30th December 1952. I have no idea what Krysia experienced during my birth, and as I have already revealed, after just two weeks, she gave up the mantle of motherhood and abandoned me. It is difficult to surmise what must have occurred during this upheaval in her life, but it is evident that for her own personal reasons, which we will never know, she was not going to play the role of a mother, consequently breaking her bond with me.

I would be lying if I said that I have never felt sad or disappointed that she did not feel able to keep me. Knowing my own joy at giving birth, it is hard to comprehend that Krysia could go through life without feeling any sense of remorse at giving me up. Perhaps, given what Krysia had already seen in her young life, she did not have any maternal instinct. On the other hand, whoever my father may have been, he too may have played a part in Krysia's ultimate decision to abandon me. Perhaps whoever he was, he was not prepared to acknowledge me. Or maybe he was never given the opportunity! As much as I have tried to search for evidence as to who my biological father may have been, it has so far eluded me.

As a mother, I find all this difficult to come to terms with. So many ifs and buts run through my mind, but whatever led Krysia to give me up, the fact remains that she was my birth mother, and I would not be writing this without her having given me life.

Chapter 18
Krysia's secrets

Krysia's decision to abandon me, for whatever reason, will remain a mystery for the rest of my life. I have spent most of my life accepting the fact that I had been abandoned by my birth mother, but I still yearned to learn more about the circumstances that led to this. I have poured over the paperwork that I received from Social Services many times, trying to find some other source of information that I may have previously overlooked. Unfortunately, I now believe that the paperwork I have is not fully complete, as there appears to be some chronological gaps. Sadly, nothing further has come to light. My cousin, Georgina, continues to be like a ferret searching for some new revelation.

The Social Services documents do show that, although there was an investigation and also a police search for Krysia, she was never found. I now know, of course, that she covered her tracks, declaring herself to be married and giving what may well be a fictitious name for my father. This resulted in the fact that she did not, in effect, sign me over officially for adoption. Consequently, until my adoption in 1958, I remained in the care of the London Council and various other institutions before finally ending up in a children's home in North Devon.

I would love to know what led to my being sent so far away from my place of birth, but again, I have resigned myself to the fact that I may never know the reason.

I have been told many times that Krysia loved children, and I know that in particular, she showered her love and affection on Richard, her nephew and godson. I have asked myself many times how she coped with carrying the inner burden of knowing that she had had a child that she never acknowledged to anyone.

After Ursula's death, I lost a vital source of information regarding Krysia. With her sister, Maria, living so far away in Kansas, I knew that it would not be easy to keep asking questions via the internet, which was our main source of communication. Maria was not very adept at writing, so I had no hope of her ever writing to me about Krysia, as Ursula had. This meant that I could not make any further substantial insight into Krysia's life.

I had learnt from Ursula that, during the celebrations of the Queen's Coronation in June 1953, Leslie Corke, Krysia's boyfriend, had driven the three of them around London, taking in the sights and displays marking this famous milestone in history. I cannot help but wonder if Krysia even gave me a passing thought as she celebrated this event. She must surely have realised that I was somewhere in the same vicinity, and how could she not have wondered how I was, a small baby of only six months of age? Such thoughts as these continue to haunt me.

However, it is apparent that Krysia continued to live her life to the full. One particular highlight for her was her marriage to Leslie Corke on 8th March 1957 at Kensington Registry Office. By coincidence, this date would prove memorable to me as it was the same date as my adopted father's birthday.

Maxymilian must have been relieved that his daughter had now become a respectably married woman. As I had been made aware by Ursula, he had not approved at all that Krysia and Leslie were living together unmarried. Yet again, I find myself tormented by the fact that Krysia remained secretive about my birth. Sadly, therefore, Maxymilian was denied the knowledge that he had a granddaughter, who would have been his first grandchild. During a conversation with Richard, I learnt that in November 1955, Maria, who was still living with her father and sister, Ursula, in the displacement camp at Fairford, had met and fallen in love with an American Serviceman, called Merle. He was based at an American Army base in the same area. Interestingly, Maria was the first bride to be married from the displacement camp, and the occasion was greeted with much excitement and celebration following the sad years of war that had been experienced by so many.

Krysia and Leslie travelled from London to celebrate Maria's nuptials. Following the wedding, Maria travelled to Kansas as a GI bride. Some six months later, she gave birth to a son. It was evident, therefore, that Maria had been pregnant when she married Merle. I am inclined to think that this revelation must surely have hit Krysia's conscience, knowing that she had a secret child.

Having been given the impression that Krysia and Leslie enjoyed a somewhat idyllic lifestyle, Barbara's words come to mind. She had told me quite often, as I was growing up, that she believed my birth parents had careers in the art and design world and that they had been part of the so-called 'Chelsea set'! Is it possible that they were indeed, just that? How would Barbara have come to this conclusion? I know that Barbara and Bill were managing the Rose and Crown pub in Hammersmith in 1952. Is it possible that they became aware of Krysia and her dilemma? Did they collude with others in order that I would eventually be removed from London to North Devon? Was there more to the reason for such a lengthy process in my eventual adoption? Once again, I find myself wondering just what my adoptive parents really knew about my birth mother. After Barbara's death, a close neighbour of mine revealed that Barbara had told her that she knew more about my circumstances than she would ever let me know. What was it, I wonder? As the years slip by, the chances of finding the true answers are becoming more and more remote.

As I have already said, Krysia and Leslie enjoyed a good lifestyle. They dined out regularly, and would often go to parties, and enjoyed extensive travel, both home and abroad. Leslie was very much in love with Krysia and showered her with gifts. One particular gift was a dachshund puppy, which Krysia named Pepe. He was an absolute favourite with Krysia, and she loved him dearly. One day, he sadly fell off their sofa and broke his back. Krysia was heartbroken, and Leslie tried to placate her by finding another dachshund to replace Pepe. But Krysia was too upset to take any interest in the new little pup. Eventually, however, being an animal lover, she could not spurn the little pup for long, and subsequently named him Pepe 2.

Leslie loved taking photographs of Krysia, and I have been fortunate enough to have several of these from Ursula and Richard that I now treasure. One photo is of Krysia standing beside Leslie's blue and cream Austin Healey, a prestigious car to own in the early 1960s. It reminds me of my own experience in my early twenties when I stood beside my one-time father-in-law's Rolls Royce. I continue to be amazed by the similarities in both our lives.

I have been repeatedly told that Krysia loved children. This irks me somewhat because, if this is the case, why did she never reveal to anyone that I existed? Or did she? I understand that Krysia had a close girlfriend whose mother was, shall we say, a call girl! Did this person know about me, and did she influence Krysia's decision to ultimately abandon me? I wish it were possible to be transported back to 1952 and have been a fly on the wall to learn just what occurred with Krysia during that year. One curious aspect of Krysia's married life was the fact that she maintained contact with her friend, Irvin Menkin. When searching on Ancestry, I discovered details of travel during 1958. Krysia and Irvin appear to have had a rendezvous in New York. Irvin sailed from Southampton to New York in March 1958, and Krysia sailed from Liverpool to New York in September of that same year. Was this purely a coincidence, or was there more to her friendship with Irvin? Why, when Krysia had married Leslie in March 1957, was she suddenly travelling all that way on her own just eighteen months later? Krysia seems to have been one intriguing lady!

Richard has told me that he liked his Uncle Leslie very much. He used to have a lot of fun with him and his sister, Ania. Krysia enjoyed the fact that, being married to a moderately wealthy man, she was able to afford to take Richard and Ania out shopping. Richard recalls that he spent many happy times being bought toys at Hamleys, the major toy shop in London. Krysia would also take him and his sister out for tea and cakes at Harrods. Ursula would often reprimand Krysia for her extravagance with the children. Richard told me that he believes it was his aunt's way of compensating for the secret child she had abandoned. He felt deep down, that Krysia was a troubled soul.

Just a few years later, Krysia's enjoyable lifestyle was to come to an abrupt end. Leslie suddenly announced that he wanted a divorce. Their love bubble had burst.

Krysia was shocked as she thought Leslie loved her, as she loved him. However, something major must have occurred that made Leslie come to such a decision to end their marriage. I cannot discover just what happened, but suffice to say, Krysia had always been a flirtatious and passionate person who enjoyed attention. Had she brought this downfall upon herself? Or had Leslie found a new love?

Unfortunately, such questions cannot be fully answered, but I did discover that Leslie later remarried!

Both Ursula and Maria have told me that Krysia was utterly heartbroken by this turn of events. Leslie had destroyed the love that Krysia thought they had between them. Or maybe, she had destroyed it. Whatever the answer is, this sad situation came to pass in the mid to late 1960s.

As if the shock of Leslie's desire for a divorce was not enough for Krysia to cope with, something far more devastating was to occur.

Krysia began to feel unwell. She dismissed the initial symptoms, believing them to be due to the misery she was experiencing from the break-up of her marriage. She chose not to tell anyone of her illness.

Once again, Krysia was keeping secrets.

Chapter 19

A journey's end

For whatever reason Leslie suddenly wanted a divorce, it resulted in Krysia finding herself without the home and the comforts that she had shared with him for several years. Although she had helped Leslie with his business, she was not a woman of substantial independent means. Leslie's request for a divorce, therefore, was a real blow. Because of their separation, it meant that she now needed to find a way of supporting herself plus somewhere to live.

Ursula was shocked at Krysia's news and invited her to stay with her and her family until she could sort out what to do next. Krysia's friends rallied around her and were sympathetic. They tried to help her as much as possible, but it was not a situation that Krysia felt comfortable about since many of her friends were Leslie's friends too! As Krysia had maintained contact with her long-time friend, Irvin Menkin, in America, she sent him word of the dilemma that had befallen her.

Irvin, was by this time living in Chicago. He was immediately sympathetic and supportive of Krysia. Deep down, from the first time they had met, he had always loved Krysia, but it was a love that had not been fully reciprocated. Despite this, Irvin was anxious to help her in any way he could, and to this end, he suggested she should join him in America.

Whilst Krysia considered this possibility; she found herself becoming increasingly unwell. Ursula sensed that Krysia was not herself and finally persuaded her to seek medical advice. Ursula accompanied Krysia on her visit to the doctor, who also happened to be a family friend. It was a shock when she was given the news that she was almost certainly suffering from cancer and needed to undergo tests. The tests proved positive; she was suffering from ovarian cancer.

Krysia found it hard to accept this diagnosis. She believed that the symptoms she had been experiencing were all due to the massive upset over the break-up of her marriage. Despite encouragement from Ursula to follow the medical regime advised for her cancer, Krysia was terrified of any intervention and steadfastly refused to undergo any treatment. Instead, she flew to Poland with Ursula to seek alternative options, but other than trying homoeopathic remedies, this proved to be futile.

Following Krysia's revelation to Irvin about the break-up of her marriage, he was anxious to see her as soon as was physically possible. Because of the distance between them, Irvin took the earliest flight possible to London to meet with her. Although they had kept in touch via letters, they had not actually seen one another for some years. There was no telling how they would feel about each other now, after such a long time.

A letter dated 5th November 1968, which has come to light through Irvin's two nieces, reveals that Irvin was nervous of meeting Krysia after such a long absence from one another. The following is a short extract from this letter, which he had written to his brother, Sam, and wife, Bernice:

"It's a good thing that I came here. To be with Teresa again was all that she or I needed. Whatever doubts we had after so long a separation vanished as soon as we saw each other. It's been a long time since I've felt so happy as I do now, and Teresa feels the same. I wish I could take her back to Chicago now, but it will be nine months or so before she can come to America - that won't seem so long now."

He goes on to talk about the many changes that he has found since he was last in London. He talks about many new buildings, the widening of streets, and a new 'subway' being under construction. He adds that the big stores are all decorated for Christmas.

I do not know why Krysia suddenly adopted the use of her second Christian name, Teresa. In a recent conversation with Irvin's nieces, I learnt that this was the name she went by with both them and their parents, Sam and Bernice Menkin.

A later passage in Irvin's letter refers to Teresa not being very well and saying that she was much worse than she had led him to believe. Irvin understood that she had been suffering from pneumonia and had been gravely ill for a few days. He goes on to say that she had regained most of the weight she had lost but that her face was still 'a bit thin'.

Given the knowledge that Krysia was suffering from cancer, I wonder whether this was the real reason for her 'illness', or was she hiding the fact that she was suffering from cancer?

Following Irvin and Krysia's reunion and the declaration of Irvin's love for Krysia, she flew out to join Irvin in Chicago the following summer of 1969.

Richard told me that he was mortified by the news that his Aunt Krysia was moving to Chicago. He said that he had missed her greatly and even went so far as to say that he felt that she had abandoned him!

From the various conversations I have had with Maria, and at one time with Ursula, I learnt that although Krysia had settled into life with Irvin in Chicago, she was keen to remain independent and to find work. She found employment at a well-known jewellery establishment in Chicago called Peacocks. I have researched this place on the internet and found that it no longer exists. However, I did discover, that it was a beautiful place to have worked, and could be compared with places such as Harrods or Fortnum and Mason. I understand from Maria that Krysia enjoyed working here very much as jewellery was a great favourite with her. I liked hearing this as I too, have a love of jewellery.

I have not been able to find any record of marriage between Irvin and Krysia, but certain paperwork, such as her passport, confirms that at some point she became Mrs. Menkin. Irvin's two nieces have told me how much they liked Krysia, or Aunt Teresa as they called her. They told me that she was a talented artist, producing several beautiful watercolours. This is something that I, too, have enjoyed as a pastime. She also had a great interest in antiques and was 'quite the expert'.

Sadly, although Krysia settled into her new life with Irvin, the spectre of her illness was still present. Added to this was the fact that she was not happy living in the vast and windy city of Chicago. It was a complete contrast to her life in London. She missed her friends and family, and despite Irvin's fervent efforts to ensure that Krysia was happy, it was a difficult situation for them both.

I feel sure that Krysia must have suffered some heartache when she learnt that Leslie had remarried in 1970. She had accepted that her marriage was over and, because there were no children involved, she did not receive any form of maintenance. I wonder to myself if this was part of the reason that Krysia readily accepted Irvin's offer to look after her, which resulted in them marrying.

Whatever the circumstances of their relationship, there is no doubt that Irvin looked after Krysia in every sense of the word. As her illness took a downward spiral, Irvin, who loved Krysia with a passion, became her carer. He devoted himself to easing Krysia's pain and discomfort as much as he was able.

Prior to Krysia's death, her sister Maria made a journey from Kansas to Chicago. She wanted to see for herself how Krysia was doing. She was shocked at how her appearance had deteriorated due to the cancer becoming more aggressive. Irvin was not at all happy by Maria's inference that she should help to look after Krysia. Irvin and Krysia had already agreed that there would be no interference from anyone for what would be Krysia's last days.

On 4th July 1973, Krysia's suffering ended. She passed away at the age of just 43, coincidently the same age as her mother had been when she died from tuberculosis in 1942.

Irvin was heartbroken. I have a copy of a letter he sent to Ursula on 8th July 1973.

This is how it reads:

Dear Ursula,

Last week was the longest week of my life - it doesn't seem possible that so much could happen in a few days. And I am sure the week seemed as long to you.

Mary (Maria) returned to Kansas a few hours after she talked to you on the telephone. Just as she did last year, Mary arrived in Chicago about an hour after Merle phoned that she was coming. At the time her plane was due to arrive, I had to be at the funeral home. Luckily, I was able to get my brother to go to the airport to pick up Mary. And I just managed to talk to Mary a few minutes after she arrived by having her paged at the airport. Sam brought her straight to the funeral home from the airport.

I'm glad now that Mary came. As you know, I was very angry with her, but one can't stay angry with Mary for very long, and I suppose that a shared sorrow brings two people closer together.

The funeral service went off better than I had hoped. Father Bill, with whom I had made the funeral arrangements on Thursday, performed the mass for Krys, and afterwards, I introduced him to Mary. Today, prayers for Krys are being offered at every mass at St. Ita's.

When I first talked with Father Bill, I asked him if it was okay to cremate Krys. He said that it was, under the circumstances. I told him that I intended to take her ashes back to England.

So Krys was cremated, and her ashes are in an urn, which is now in a vault at the cemetery. I plan to go to

London early next year, and I shall take the urn with me. In London, I will do whatever you wish. We can either put the ashes in a crypt or strew them somewhere in England where Krys was happy. Or even take the ashes to Poland. I know you would have preferred that Krys be buried, but I hope you understand my reasons, as Mary did.

A few people from Peacock's showed up, and Mr. Tesar, the boss, came in for a few minutes on Friday evening when visitors were permitted at the funeral home. I kept the casket closed during the visitation period.

By the time you receive this letter your holiday will be almost over, unless it takes less time for this to reach you than I expect. I hope that you let yourself enjoy your visit to Poland. I telephoned you yesterday both because Mary was here and to sort of ease your mind about the last rites for Krys.

After the funeral, I brought Mary here, and we spent several hours together (Mary slept at Sam's house on Friday night). I filled a suitcase with some of Krys's things (winter coats, boots, sweaters, etc.), and Mary took them with her to Kansas. I'm going to gradually send all of Krys's clothing to Mary - a box every week or so - since she can make good use of most of it.

Sam and Bernice took Mary to the airport, and of course, I went along with them. I promised Mary, just as I had promised you, that I would continue to feel that I was part of the family.

Bernice and Sam send their love, Love to everyone ... Signed Irvin.

When I had finished reading this letter, I had a lump in my throat. I was very sad at the thought that Krysia should have passed away like this. Her life had not only been cut short, but it had also been a roller-coaster of emotions and experiences.

Her early life was overshadowed by the despair of war. The loss of her mother just as she approached her teenage years was a big shock. This was followed by an incredible journey across the world in the midst of war with her two sisters. After the war, she finally found a sense of peace with her new life in England. Then came the initial rush of finding love and happiness with Leslie. The loss of that love some years later shook her greatly. To find herself on her own once more must have taken its toll. The unbelievable news that she had cancer was the final straw. I can't help but feel that life had not been entirely fair to her. Some people go through life with barely any upset, while others seem to have an unfair share of it. Krysia's final years were thankfully spent in the company of Irvin, who truly cared for her. This at least is a comfort, knowing that Krysia's last months were eased as far as possible by Irvin and his unstinting devotion to her.

My one abiding sadness of all that came to pass is that Krysia never found it within her heart to acknowledge me to anyone.

There was just one final journey for Krysia, albeit she would not be aware of it. Irvin arranged to bring Krysia's ashes to England, and in agreement with Krysia's family, her ashes were placed in the Columbarium Niche at Breakspear Crematorium, Ruislip.

So Irvin had completed his duty to Krysia, but where did this leave him? He was truly bereft at the loss of Krysia. He had waited so long to have her in his life, only to lose her just a few short years later. Irvin was a very quiet, loving man. I discovered from his nieces that he wrote for the US Army newspaper, Stars and Stripes. He also wrote poems, articles about meteorology, and current events. He had a very intellectual curiosity and a wide range of knowledge. Krysia's death made him reconsider what he wanted to do with his life. He decided to leave Chicago and took an apartment in Ealing to be close to Krysia's sister, Ursula, and her family. He got on well with Ursula, and her husband, Boleslaw. He also enjoyed the company of their children, Richard and Ania. Together they all shared the loss of Krysia, who had been a very special person in their lives. Richard recalls how he and his family took Irvin on the train to Canterbury. Irvin had a keen interest in seeing the historical sights of England. He was fascinated by Canterbury's magnificent Cathedral. In the late summer of 1977, Irvin decided to undertake a tour of Europe.

What no one could have foreseen was that it was a tour he would never return from. After arriving at the train station in Copenhagen, Irvin stepped off the train, promptly collapsed, and died from a massive heart attack. It was a shock for his brother Sam who, having been informed of Irvin's death, immediately flew from America to Copenhagen. He was accompanied by his wife, Bernice. Irvin was cremated during a small service at Mariebjerg Crematorium in Copenhagen. His ashes were then brought to England in December 1977 to be placed alongside Krysia's ashes at the Breakspear Crematorium.

Both Krysia's and Irvin's ashes remained here until October 2012, when they were removed for collection by Ursula and her family. Later, Richard undertook to be custodian of their ashes. After the revelation that I was Krysia's secret daughter, Richard asked me if

I would like to have my birth mother's ashes. My response was an immediate yes, to which Richard then suggested I might also like to have Irvin's ashes in order that they would remain together. So it is that I now have their ashes in my care until such time as I finally decide what to do with them. I intend to consult with Richard and Irvin's two nieces when making this decision.

And so, my story draws to a close. It has been a real eye-opener in many ways, and I will be forever grateful to my cousin, Georgina, for her unstinting sleuthing, together with her enthusiasm in urging me to find my birth family.

I regard myself as extremely fortunate to have been accepted immediately with love and kindness by my birth family, despite their initial shock at my existence.

My husband, Jeff, has been a constant support in my quest to write this, and my son, Liam, has been equally supportive.

Now my mind turns to finding who my birth father is or was, but I fear that this will be a less successful task.

I have an enormous amount to be grateful for in my life, and I have been enriched by the knowledge and the people I have come to know through my search.

Epilogue - What happened next

If someone had told me when I was first adopted in 1958 that I would stand beside my maternal grandfather's grave some sixty years later, I would never have believed them. But this is just where I found myself in November 2018.

After the excitement of finding my birth family in 2017, Richard took me to Poland to see where my birth mother and her family had lived.

The two and half hour journey by plane was pleasant, and all the time, I was pinching myself that this was really happening. We landed at Lech Walesa Gdańsk Airport, and before long, we were outside where I caught my first sight of Poland. It was quite unlike anything I had envisioned. There was no great hustle and bustle of people or traffic. Richard had hired a car, and we drove through very grey and misty weather to the medieval town of Toruń. As we drove, my view was of long stretches of barren fields of dark soil. There were many forests of fir trees, standing tall and stark against the grey skyline; everything appeared dismal in appearance. My mind was filled with the horrors that those forests had witnessed during the war. It was quite a poignant moment for me.

I learnt that the town of Torun was the birthplace of the great 16th-century astronomer, Mikolaj (Nicholas)

Copernicus. I was very happy that we were going to stay overnight in this beautiful town. It was a very attractive place with cobbled streets and tall, Gothic-looking ornate red brick buildings. We went to a local restaurant, where I had my first taste of Barszcz (beetroot soup). It was delicious, warming, and thoroughly enjoyable. I also enjoyed eating a variety of Pierogi (stuffed dumplings), Poland's national favourite dish. Richard and I later walked back to the hotel and, on our way, sampled some traditional gingerbread from the town's own bakery. The excitement of the day made it very easy for me to fall asleep that night. The following day we set off for the town of Inowraclaw, where the family had lived. I felt deeply emotional when Richard took me to visit my grandfather's grave - without whom I would not exist. From the small shop at the entrance to the cemetery's gates, I chose a candle jar with a red heart on it to place at Maxymilian 's grave. I could hardly believe that I was finally standing in front of the person who was responsible for my origin. It was a surreal moment as Richard and I stood at his grave. We held hands and gazed at the memorial stone, and both of us had tears in our eyes. I really appreciated being able to pay my respects to my birth mother's father. I hope, in the future, that I will return.

After visiting Inowraclaw we journeyed to Gdan'sk, where we stayed for the rest of our time. Richard showed me many beautiful sights, and I enjoyed lots of traditional Polish food. I felt very privileged that I had been able to gain such an amazing insight into my heritage. My visit to Poland was an incredible experience.

On my arrival back home, my mind was so full of memories that I wrote a diary of my time in Poland.

There had been so much to see that I wanted to commit it to paper.

In early 2019, an article in the Daily Mail highlighted the upsurge of people searching for long lost families through Ancestry DNA. The article asked for anyone who had experience with this to write in. I wrote about my search and was surprised to find myself being invited to travel to the Daily Mail offices in London for an interview.

Because I had recently suffered another TIA, Jeff was cautious about me travelling on my own. He was not well himself, so could not accompany me. A good friend came to my rescue and agreed to travel with me. In June 2019, we set off for London by train. On arrival at the offices of the Daily Mail, I was immediately whisked away to have my hair and make-up done in preparation for a photoshoot. To my surprise, I was even given an outfit to wear for the shoot. It was like being a star for a day!

Linda Kelsey conducted the interview with me in a quiet room away from the hustle and bustle of the offices. She was fascinated by my tale. She seemed surprised that I bore no malice toward my birth mother for giving me up. I told her that I could not condemn her when I had no knowledge of the reason why she chose to abandon me. My story was to appear in the paper in the following few weeks. I couldn't believe that I was going to appear in a national newspaper. I half hoped that it might trigger someone's memory and lead to me finding out more about my birth mother or even revealing some evidence about my father. The article was published on my son's birthday, 15th July, which I thought was an amazing coincidence. Filled with excitement, I bought half a dozen copies of the paper that day to send to friends and relatives. Sadly, it brought very little attention from anyone, and nothing new came to light. It was, however, my five minutes of fame!

The following month I finally met with my American cousin, Roger, and his wife, Kathy. They were in London for a couple of nights as part of their European tour. We arranged to meet at the Tate Modern, with Richard and his son Alex joining us. It was a wonderful moment as we all sat down for a meal in the restaurant. As we dined, Roger ordered a bottle of champagne to toast the reuniting of long-lost cousins. I was amazed at the similarity between Roger and Richard; they could almost have been brothers. There was certainly a strong family resemblance between us all. Once again, my emotions were rocked by this momentous occasion.

I continue to stay in touch with all the members of my newfound family. I feel blessed too, that the family that Barbara and Bill brought me into all those years ago are just as special to me now as they always were.

Just recently, I decided to contact members of Irvin's family and, to my delight, found his two nieces, Marcy and Judy. I had no idea how they would accept my intrusion on their lives, and I was touched by their immediate warmth and friendship towards me. It has been lovely to gain more knowledge about Irvin and the relationship between him and Krysia. I can't help but think that, had things been different, I could have been Irvin's stepdaughter!

And so, from a tentative start to my journey of discovering who my birth mother was, I have truly come a long way.

Who knows what there is yet to discover? I wait in anticipation...